Praise for
Path of the Moonlit Hedge

"Nathan's work offers practical, lifeway-building rituals, meditations, and tools to inspire and guide those interested in reclaiming the universal mantle of animist into their spiritual life...He beautifully brings us back to center to ponder the magic of the simple flame engulfing the candle wick and springing to life, mirroring, as above, so below, the universe and all their awe-inspiring mystery. He also does not skip over important issues such as systemic racism and the challenges faced by queer and trans people while walking this way. A wonderful work."

—Rebecca Beyer, author of *Wild Witchcraft*

"Combining folklore, personal experience, several rabbit holes' worth of research, and a dash of popular culture, *The Path of the Moonlit Hedge* is unlike any other hedgewitchery book I've seen. The author uses narratives from their own life, from history, from fable and parable, and so the work of hedgecraft feels like spending time poking at a bramble thicket border with someone who knows what they're looking for."

—Cory Thomas Hutcheson, author of *New World Witchery*

"An illuminating exploration into the world of animism and witchcraft. Not only does it provide an incredibly in-depth and thoughtful exploration of animism in a witchcraft context, but it also provides unique and insightful perspectives on the subject...This book is sure to expand your tool kit of connection through its many wonderful exercises and give you a better understanding of the power of animism."

—Mat Auryn, bestselling author of *Psychic Witch*

"*The Path of the Moonlit Hedge* follows Nathan's journey of healing and transformation to become enmeshed with the life of nature and the calling of his soul. The insights, techniques, and rituals he shares are the summation of his experience and are new and meant for this new era. At the same time, the blood of the ancients informs this book, and the timeless hands of many spirits have touched this work. If you are looking to refresh your connection to the primal powers or begin the work for the first time, *The Path of the Moonlit Hedge* will serve you well."

—Ivo Dominguez Jr., author of *Four Elements of the Wise*

"An important guide for self-care and personal development… This book, geared for the newcomer and long-term practitioner alike, will help you to create daily practices that are rooted in the power and stability of the natural world."

—Rev. Wendy Van Allen, author of *Relighting the Cauldron*

"A book for anyone and everyone who is interested in animism, witchcraft, and the intersection and relationships between them...A beautifully written book with pure magic in its pages!"

—Emma Kathryn, author of *Witch Life*

"Nathan Hall's *Path of the Moonlit Hedge* is personal, practical, and downright powerful. Nathan is a spirited storyteller who guides the reader on a path of partnering with the natural world to build resilience, heal the soul, and ignite one›s inner magic."

—Nicholas Pearson, author of *Crystal Basics* and *Flower Essences from the Witch's Garden*

"With a writing style as witty and informative as it is accessible, *The Path of the Moonlit Hedge* is a gift to those who wish to delve deeper into their magical practice. Loaded with practical exercises and stories from the author's life, this book makes available what has often been obscured: the philosophies and techniques of shifting our consciousness so that we may free ourselves from the death-grip of the ego and learn to hear the whisperings of the natural world all around us."

—Storm Faerywolf, author of *Betwixt & Between*

Path of the
MOONLIT HEDGE

Foreword by Christopher Penczak

Path of the
MOONLIT
HEDGE

Discovering the Magick of
Animistic Witchcraft

Nathan M. Hall

Llewellyn Publications • Woodbury, Minnesota

FIRST EDITION
First Printing, 2023

Book design by Mandie Brasington
Cover design by Kevin R. Brown
Editing by Laura Kurtz
Sigil illustrations on pages 65, 66 and 67 by Llewellyn Art Department

Llewellyn Publications is a registered trademark of Llewellyn Worldwide Ltd.

Library of Congress Cataloging-in-Publication Data (Pending)
ISBN: 978-0-7387-7273-8

Llewellyn Worldwide Ltd. does not participate in, endorse, or have any authority or responsibility concerning private business transactions between our authors and the public.

All mail addressed to the author is forwarded but the publisher cannot, unless specifically instructed by the author, give out an address or phone number.

Any internet references contained in this work are current at publication time, but the publisher cannot guarantee that a specific location will continue to be maintained. Please refer to the publisher's website for links to authors' websites and other sources.

Llewellyn Publications
A Division of Llewellyn Worldwide Ltd.
2143 Woodddale Drive
Woodbury, MN 55125-2989
www.llewellyn.com

Printed in the United States of America

© Sarah Knudtson

About the Author

Nathan Hall is a witch, animist, initiate of the Anderson Feri Tradition and member of the Temple of Witchcraft. He serves on the board of the annual Mystic South Conference and is a contributor and editorial advisor for The Wild Hunt, a daily news source for the Pagan community. Nathan has two decades of experience working as a journalist and editor, has lectured at media conferences, and has sat on a variety of panels.

For Lucien, for a better and more awakened humanity.

Contents

Exercises

Acknowledgments

This is my first published book. While I've written book-length things before, managing to get one completed and out into the daylight could not have been done without the help and support of a number of people.

First and foremost, my wife, Juliette, who has generously given me the time and patience needed to produce it. Your encouragement and support were absolutely essential to my success. "Always for love."

I'd like to thank my editor, Heather Greene, for her enthusiastic support of my work, dating back to our time at The Wild Hunt together. For years, she encouraged me to pitch her something, and I finally did!

I'd also like to thank my friend and teacher, Christopher Blackthorn, who contributed so much to my spiritual development and challenged me to think differently about what witchcraft is and could be. My black heart is feral and free. We are shining, and we will never be afraid again!

Christopher Penczak, thank you for being an important mentor and teacher. I had been practicing for many, many years before I started in the Mystery School in the Temple of Witchcraft, which finally helped me in so many ways gather up all my disparate ducks and put them in a line. Thank you for your love, will and wisdom.

Nicholas Pearson-Walsh, I don't know what I would have done without your advice at the start of writing this! You're such a caring and generous soul, a humble rock star! Thank you!

And to my "witch-husband," Michael, who keeps me informed about things in the outside world, challenges my preconceptions, and keeps me laughing.

Thank you to my sister and all my friends who have seen me through this process, keeping me sane and grounded by sending me missives in my primary form of communication: memes.

Foreword
by Christopher Penczak

Do you remember that first night where you walked under the moonlight in some semi-wild place where perhaps you shouldn't have been? Whether you were alone or with another, there was a current of excitement, a thrill of the unknown coursing through your body. On one hand, such a moment is filled with this sense of illicit discovery—you are doing something most people do not. You are walking an edge. On the other hand, perhaps the unconscious realization that this is what should be, and walking in the wild under the full moon is the natural state of all humans. We have simply forgotten.

I remember my first moonlit walk with a thrill that, at the time, I could not articulate. I had not quite hit puberty but was old enough to find the world and all of our roles, responsibilities, and relationships quite complex and confusing. In our neighborhood, the archetypal neighborhood of the 1980s where kids played outside all summer until the streetlights came on (now popularized in the nostalgia of shows like Stranger Things), our group would go back out after supper when the moon was full. We played a nocturnal game of kick the can. For those unfamiliar, the game is a bit of a Frankenstein's monster of a game, being part tag, part hide-and-seek, and part capture the flag. Being at night, we of course would go hide in the edges of the woods behind our suburban houses and wait for our opportunity to run out and win, listening in the dark for our fellow players. And when we listened, we would hear other things too. It was during those nights when we hid that I realized the mystery of the world at the edge of the forest.

Of course we played in the woods by day, finding small snakes and rummaging through the swamps. We would "help" by destroying infestations of tent caterpillars with a local Boy Scout troop leader and make our stick forts. Occasionally we'd find burnt out campfires of the older kids drinking and partying in the woods and can see now how they too, with their hidden woodland parties, were seeking something primal and missing in our modern society, lacking meaningful rites of passage into adulthood. It was in those woods and fields where we would play wizard and witch, gathering ingredients for our spells and potions. But it was in the dark nights where you might hear things that you could not easily identify: the rustle of a not-so-small creature, the call of a nightbird, and even a surprised deer running away from you. You became aware of how everything was alive, and you felt like everything was watching you, though most things didn't necessarily care about you. You were simply there, something unusual for the creatures who normally dwelled in the dark to take notice. This world did not center upon you.

It was in the dark that I found myself suddenly face-to-face with a giant spider web and the shiny spider in its center—luckily stopping myself before stepping into it. I was equally fascinated and freaked out, the awe found at the double edge of fear and fascination. I stared at it gleaming in the moonlight for quite a while before I brought myself back to the game. Summer vacations and running in the woods in both daylight and darkness brought an education that, though quite different from the rest of our school year, was just as valuable.

Not that many years later, I had another moonlight adventure that started another important educational journey. While not in the woods, and in truth not that far away from where we played those nocturnal games, I was invited to be a guest at a local coven's full moon esbat. While perhaps a less formal and likely thing today with the growing community of Witches in the world, at the time, like a child walking alone in the woods at night, it was a somewhat illicit affair. At the time, it was secretive and formal, and quite a big deal. It represented a great deal of trust and was not an opportunity offered lightly.

While it was in someone's otherwise ordinary backyard, when we started it might has well been a clearing in the deep woods, a mountaintop in Germany, a stone circle in England, or the opening of a cave in Spain. The plants, trees, stones, and Witches shimmered under the silvery light and the glow of a few candles and lanterns hung in the four quarters. In many ways, I was a child again in the dark, face-to-face with the spider in its web, but this time the spider was the mystery of the Witch Goddess as embodied by the high priestess. Despite my skeptical nature, I couldn't help but be enthralled. When she raised her hands to call to the moon, the clouds parted to reveal the full moon, giving everything a silvery white glow. When the rite was concluded and she said farewell to the moon, the clouds gathered again, and we were illuminated by only the remaining candles.

In reading Nathan Hall's first book, now in your hands, I am reminded quite a bit about both those experiences and how they have led to so many of the changes in my life and worldview, great and small. While Nathan does not personally take you into the darkness for a game or to the formal ritual circle of a coven, he invites you to seek these mysteries in your own way. The animist world view reinforces the idea that everything is alive and aware with consciousness. While showing you key fundamentals if it is your first journey walking next to or jumping over the moonlit hedge, his deconstructionist (really, decompositional) attitude is like the forest with its continual cycles of breaking things down and growing new things. Nathan looks at the things around us in the seemingly objective world, through the observation of nature and takes you on some unique explorations, such as his mushroom magickal talisman, as well as the forces with us in terms of our own personal consciousness, our souls, and the process to align and reorder our perceptions and consciousness. Art becomes key to shifting these perceptions to explore and experience yourself. His work encourages you to get outside and experience your place, time, environment, and most importantly, your relationship to it. And for those of us in lands having more archetypal four seasons and rhythms more common to classical Witch folklore (such as my own home in New England), his experience and home life in Florida encourages us all to look outside of those familiar Wheel of the Year stories to relate to who and what lives in your own area. In going outside, we also learn to go inside and reflect upon ourselves beyond linear time and rational thinking, to a sense of enchantment and wonder that I know I found in the dark under the moon. Lastly, he leads us into the world of spirit, rooted in but adjacent to our wild world of nature and our own inner consciousness.

Don't simply read this book. Experience. Answer the invitation to go outside, to go inside, and to go over the moonlit hedge.

Christopher Penczak
November 2022
Salem, NH

Christopher Penczak is the co-founder of the Temple of Witchcraft tradition and nonprofit organization based in New Hampshire with world wide membership. He is the author of the award winning *Temple of Witchcraft* series of books and recordings, as well as the co-owner of Copper Cauldron Publications. Christopher primarily serves as a minister in the Witchcraft and LGBTQIA communities by maintaining a healing practice, teaching schedule, and leading small retreats to sacred sites.

Introduction

Let's begin with a garden. Lush and green, you can look across an expanse and see every variety of flower, vegetable, and some fruit trees in the far corners. A beautiful live oak shades the center and offers an anchor. A reflecting pool feeds a gentle, bubbling stream that flows off and out of the garden. Surrounding this tranquil scene is a hedgerow of bay laurel, and as the sun sets and the full moon rises, the leaves gently reflect the glow of moonlight, lending an ethereal, almost hazy effect.

When we approach the hedge, we see that it's not entirely there at all, as if its substance is both here and not here. We could walk right through if we choose, but where would we end up? And would we be able to return? Would we be the same or irrevocably changed by the process?

This is where your journey begins. This will be your home for this experience and will be a place you can return to frequently to recharge, reset or embark on your next adventure. It's a place of peace and meditation, a sojourn from the modern world which provides many portals for you to explore. And while this garden is an inviolable place of safety, the hedge that you cross from here provide risk and reward. They provide opportunities for healing and growth and interaction with your own demons, land spirits, the gods, and ancestors.

We are living in interesting times. We are living in challenging times. We are living in magickal times. Never before has humanity, as far as we know, gone through an epoch quite like the one we're experiencing right at this moment. Some see it as a great opportunity, the front-row seat for observing the next phase of humanity in whatever form it takes. The incredible part is that you get to choose your own contribution to this era. What will you contribute? How will you aid humanity and the planet that birthed you? It's exciting, challenging, and overwhelming. Horror and awe in equal measures are appropriate reactions. This era is a blessing and a curse for those of us who are living through it. And obviously, the younger you are, the more of it you'll receive. As a father, it is distressing but I also have to accept the reality on the ground: climate change, political polarization, a whole encyclopedia of -isms, billionaire and millionaire classes with their mostly clueless children inheriting it all, and working people struggling to survive a system they didn't create and which largely doesn't benefit them. It doesn't sound all that fun, but with change comes possibility, and I encourage the magickal folk who read this book to keep that in mind and gear your magick where it's needed most: in defense of the earth and its denizens and a new path forward for humanity. As occultists, magicians, and witches, this is the time to cultivate and use our gifts and talents.

A Swelling Tide

When it comes to my craft, my approach is, in a word, animistic. We'll delve more into animism later but briefly, animism is the philosophy and belief that the universe and all of its inhabitants are imbued each with their own animating spirit or soul. When I started writing, there were few craft books I had been exposed to that covered the topic. Over the course of my study, a raft of new titles were released that touch on different aspects of animism. It was pleasing to see because I sincerely believe that this spiritual and philosophical approach is essential for our species to survive and take our next evolutionary steps on a changing planet.

There's also a lot in this book about healing work. People are in crisis right now, things are changing faster than we can adapt, and everyone in one way or another is feeling the burden of it. The heart of my witchcraft (and witchcraft in general in my opinion), is healing ourselves in order to be the most self-possessed version we can be. Self-possession is empowerment and whether that allows you to be the best healer, changer of fate, a mystic seer, or in whatever way you are able to contribute, your contributions are now requested and required. Doing the work that allows you to fully embrace this is vitally important.

Working alongside the countless spirits that inhabit where you live is another key factor to creating the change we seek. For too long, humanity has excused itself from the rhythms of the natural world, from forging friendships and alliances with land spirits in order to work together. We'll endeavor to places natural and strange and seek deeper relationships and begin the work of reorienting ourselves and humanity's place within the universe.

Finally, we'll explore the unique and powerful initiatory experience of the witches' sabbat, more fully committing to the work we've taken on.

What Does This Book Offer?

I have done the exercises, meditations, and other workings included in this book; they have improved my life and, more importantly, made me more resilient to the grand upheaval that we're all experiencing. So I'm bringing it all to you in the sincere and humble hope that you will get the same from it.

This book is loaded with new workings I've created myself, and there are also many exercises that will be familiar to those who have spent some time studying the craft. I felt it was important to include both for those who might be new to these concepts. You can skip ahead if you're familiar, but as every person's practice is different, I encourage you to read through and see if there might be even a small part that's new and usable to you.

I'm excited to share this experience with you and hope you get as much out of it as I have and do. Magick is the wondrous inheritance of humanity, and I firmly believe that we are living in an epoch in which it will become more apparent. Blessings on your journey down the crooked path of the witch!

1.

Hedgewalking, Witchcraft, and Animism

Walking the hedges is not for everyone; even showing interest in this path reveals that you may actually have some aptitude for it. Being a hedgewalker is a decision and not an easy one because it means to fully embrace the oddities and peculiarities that most people spend a lifetime trying to hide or eliminate. This can lead to all manner of personality and energetic schisms that divert our energy and attention. True healing and balance is an ongoing project that most of us in spiritual communities at least say we want to achieve but the hedgewalker knows that there is no straight line. Instead, they attempt to use the information collected along the way to assist themselves and others.

Adopting the label of "hedgewalker" can be perilous. Labels are humans' attempt to more clearly identify things in the world so that we know how to organize them. It's great for sorting and organizing different species of plants and animals, attributes of stones, classifications of stars, and all manner of other things. People, on the other hand, are a bit more complicated or at the very least, the labels we've inherited are no longer adequate for classification as our species continues to grow and recognize all kinds of new things about itself that actually were there all along.

Selecting a label, a name, a title, and so on should be done with careful consideration because of the energetic resonance that assuming such a role carries with it. Quickly adopting and discarding labels may signal a lack of maturity, which is fine! Everyone goes through phases where they try things and experiment in order to figure out who they are or want to be! A normal part of being a young person is experimenting with identity, if this describes who and where you are right now, embrace it.

There can be an inherent danger in frequent adoption of and discarding labels that may increase the possibility of creating a fractured personality, especially as you grow older. Fortunately, there are safe ways and safe spaces for play and discovery.

Hedgewalking

The term "hedgewalker" often brings to mind associations with green forms of witchcraft (herbalism especially) and a sense of partnership with nature and nature spirits. All of this is part of my regular practice, but there's another layer of context that I and others have adopted. When I say "hedgewalking," I'm talking about existing at the margins. Humanity has always benefited from those who have chosen to live at the edges of human experience. Think of Prometheus, crossing the veil to steal fire from the gods and bring it back for the betterment of our species. Hedgewalkers participate in that same Promethean tradition to help others in their community as well as deepen their own understanding of themselves and the universe. Shamans, medicine women and men, fairy doctors, mambos and houngans, village healers and more have historically been associated with these roles. By the way, as a word of warning, you may want to read up about how Prometheus's efforts served him if you're unfamiliar. Hedgewalkers can sometimes find themselves on the short end of the stick at the end.

In that same vein, queer people, trans folk, as well as BIPOC (Black, Indigenous and people of color) have experience with crossing the boundaries our society has manufactured. The concept of code switching—where people will change their style of speech, mannerisms, appearance and behavior to make other (often white) people more comfortable—is one example. The term itself originated in the academic study of linguistics to define the free switching between two or more languages that frequently happens in bilingual (or even multilingual) communities, which could be seen as a sort of hedge-riding of its own.[1]

People who are more comfortable, or at least, familiar, with the practice of existing in multiple worlds might discover that hedgewalking witchcraft feels suited to them and that's great. But hedgewalking, as mentioned earlier, is also about dipping into the places where few actually go or would even reasonably want to go. Let's be honest, it's a very small part of the Pagan community (to say nothing of the population at large) who have the curiosity, bravery, and foolish self-confidence in equal measure to endeavor into the world of spirits, gods, and the dead. For those who do, it's akin to starting the journey of the Fool in the traditional tarot deck and going backwards to end the journey as the Magician. You need to be both when venturing into the liminal. Over time it becomes easier, especially if you work on staying spiritually clean, working through complexes, and healing and restoring the damaged parts of yourself.

The Liminal

"The liminal" (or "liminality") is one of those terms that's become a bit of a buzzword in recent years. Meant to define a space that is neither here nor there, it's both—the hazy boundary where the ocean and the land kiss, where the mountain meets the sky, where the forest turns to mist...where lovers' lips first meet.

As the latest phase in witchcraft popularity arose, a preoccupation with liminality came with it. For whatever the reasons, it's important to pay attention when cultural zeitgeists emerge because it often indicates something that's not being addressed in the overculture. Each generation that finds resonance with the term witchcraft brings with them their own definitions and flavors that define how they view and practice it and what the world sorely needs. Liminality was something needed by this generation, and it's really no surprise why. Bringing the liminal to the forefront is almost the calling sign for people who are inheriting a society that has clearly and unapologetically

---

1. Danica Salazar, "Switching gears: revising code-switching, n.," Oxford English Dictionary (blog), https://public.oed.com/blog/revising-code-switching/. Retrieved July 28, 2022.

shut out so many. The liminal is the well of human creativity, where our concepts are challenged and changed; it is the cauldron of the witch, Cerridwen's cauldron of Awen, where we may be reborn, where metamorphosis happens. This is the place where real magick happens and it is awe-ful and inspiring, dangerous and deadly. All in a day's work then, right?

As you read and practice along with this book, keep in mind: if you feel like you're in over your head, it's best to back up and practice where you're at for a while instead of pushing through.

At the heart of hedgewalking, we meet the liminal. But why witchcraft?

Witchcraft

When I spoke with my personal guides and spiritual mentors, they made it clear that the term "witch" is an evolutionary and at times revolutionary epithet that needs to be nurtured and not discarded. It's hard to imagine it being revolutionary now with it having been so mainstreamed, but it was and, in some ways, remains so. Where we are now as witches is definitely a more evolutionary period, one that is very important and potentially building toward a period of greater prominence and influence on humanity's fate in the coming decades.

With that being said, the term "witch" exists in countless forms and has countless meanings. What does it mean to be a witch? Is it different in New Orleans than New York? And how is it different in Kenya or India? For much of human history, to be labeled a witch was akin to a death sentence and continues to be so in much of the world. Don't be lulled into thinking that just because you can find witchcraft books at Walmart, embracing the term is not a big choice, even in places like Europe, Australia, or the United States where it's relatively safer to adopt the title.

For myself, "witch" is a term that I eventually embraced after a lot of trepidation. After all, how was what I was doing significantly different from practices I'd seen others do who simply called themselves Pagan or druid? I think the answer is that I just felt like a witch. It resonated and felt powerful in a way that other things did not. When I allowed myself to embrace the moniker, it was empowering, liberating ... and even thrilling!

At various times and through many explorations of esoteric subjects, I felt compelled to set aside witch as either not feeling very serious, or being unnecessarily confrontational but I never did because of its seemingly limitless potential for growth. In many ways, it is still a wild vine bearing exotic fruit that can heal and harm depending on what is called for. Witches are the wild world speaking through humanity. Hedgewitches infinitely more so.

Animism

This brings us around to another slowly building cultural concept: animism. As I write this, I'm watching a steady stream of new books coming out on the topic. It brings so much joy to my black heart to see the era of arch tech bros be met with something bigger. Facebook's Meta may offer an infinite experience, but it will always be a sad little world filled with manipulative algorithms. Compare it with the one we repeatedly abuse and discard, the one filled with infinite spirits, gods, humans, banana slugs, fey, barrow wights, cats, cacao trees, waterbears, etc. We're all atoms in a truly incomprehensibly massive … thing … that most of us call the universe but some of us call the Goddess, the Star Goddess, the All that Is, or if you're a Discordian, the Void which spawns Eris and Aneris.

If we are the wild world speaking through humanity, animism is the voice and the spirit behind that voice. Many friends and fellow practitioners have been talking about animism for a long time; it's not new, in fact it may describe the oldest religious or spiritual impulse that visited humanity.

Göbekli Tepe is one such place where we can see the ancient influence of animism. Located in present day eastern Turkey, Göbekli Tepe was, as best as we can discern, an ancient ceremonial site, indeed one of the oldest ever discovered.[2] It's filled with towering statues of animals and is constructed in alignment with certain stellar markers indicating a culture that in all likelihood was transitioning from hunter/gatherer toward urbanization, bringing the spirits of animals, the land, and the sky with them.

Jump forward a few dozen millennia to the colonial era, where the newly formed social science called anthropology called animism a very primitive

---

2. UNESCO World Heritage Convention, "Göbekli Tepe," accessed August 2, 2022, https://whc.unesco.org/en/list/1572/.

way of understanding and making sense of how the world worked. It was seen as little more than anthropomorphizing the physical world in order to understand its processes. Why did the river flood? River spirits were not properly appeased and given sacrifice. Why did the crops fail? The land clearly did not accept the virgin we offered to it. While there is much to be discussed in a later chapter about sacrifice, this sort of simplistic treatment is just plainly inaccurate and insulting to practicing animists. It's the sort of nonsense that Europeans promoted in their world conquest to justify a lot of bad atrocities.

Animism is the belief that every living thing is inherently enspirited or ensouled. Many, if not most, animists would also argue that everything in the universe, whether recognized as biologically alive or not, is also imbued with spirit. Rocks, rivers, televisions, Neptune, even (gods forbid) PT Cruisers. The field theory of consciousness touches on this a bit and is worth reading more on if you're interested in getting into some really egg-headed stuff but it states that every particle in the universe contains a spark of what we would call consciousness.

Moreover, as we are all equally instilled with spirit, we are capable of communicating, befriending, seeking favors from, or having disagreements with any such equally enspirited beings. Animism is the act of creating relationships with beings who aren't human. You are not a machine interacting with dumb objects in a lifeless world—you are a spark of divinity experiencing itself, and at the end of your life you will have all the materials that make up your self-move and manifest in new ways.

It is the opposite of materialism. It is a remedy to the soul-wound of capitalism.

Common Misconceptions about Animism

Here are a few common misconceptions that people have around about animism.

- Animists can't work with [deity name].

  False. Animism is a worldview that informs how you interact with the world around you and potentially changes your values both materially and spiritually (I say "potentially" because perhaps you already do see the world this way but were never introduced to the term). In my practice, deities (among other powerful spirits) are active in my every day. I don't worship them, I work with them, but everyone has their own kinks. If adulation is what works for you and your gods, then that's what's good for you.

- Animism should be a closed practice.

To restate: Animism is a worldview that informs how you interact with the world and how you value things materially and spiritually. It belongs to everyone and is likely the earliest form of spiritual expression of humanity. There are countless cultures that presently have an animist worldview that are unique and sometimes sacred to them. Don't appropriate their cultures, customs or practices because that is, in fact, icky, and should be avoided. Learning about others and especially learning *from* others is human nature though, and while culture is always co-created, theft is another matter entirely.

- Animism is just a way to make shamanism acceptable for white people to practice.

Shamanism has its place in the world and I know a number of people who practice it in one form or another. There are certainly negatives concerning the way the word has been picked up in popular culture and in the way that New Agers and Pagans have used it historically and even currently without reference to its origins.

That being said, there has been a lot of careful work done to right some of the wrongs of the past and reputable shamanic schools and practitioners have worked hard to be at the front of this, owning the mistakes and attempting to atone for them. There are also good arguments, however, that the term is too often applied as a catch-all for indigenous practices around the world thfat in spite of their similarities, have no cohesive connection with one another and thus is an attempt at homogenization that robs cultures of their uniqueness.[3]

---

3. Billy-Ray Bellcourt, "Fatal Naming Rituals," *Hazlitt*, July 19, 2018, https://hazlitt.net/feature/fatal-naming-rituals.

Returning to the original question though, no, animism is not shamanism in new clothes. While some practices may look similar or overlap, my animism informs my witchcraft. It is a core worldview that dictates how I practice my spirituality.

Animism as Healing

Animism might also be the one thing that can save humanity from itself and reshape how our species views its place in relation to the rest of the universe. Giving land, rivers or ecosystems the same legal rights as people,[4] as has been done in several countries around the world in recent years, is one small step towards this. It's not enough and it might not be for the best reasons in every instance, but it's progress and in an age that can safely be characterized as reactionary and nihilistic, it's a flower growing in the proverbial pile of dung.

If you're not talking to the plants growing around you or the wild animals seen in your ecosystem, it's time to begin. There's a tendency in a lot of witchcraft to view these creatures as symbols, guideposts, or divinatory aides. Popular questions on message boards like Reddit still include the "What does it mean when I see a hawk?" variety. And sometimes the answer is that you live in a hawk's ecosystem and it's flying around doing hawk stuff, not giving answers to your relationship problems. It's best to assume that the creature with its own agency and needs is working on those things first and scale up from there. I will get to what it means when you do see sacred animals and what that means, but the theme that all animals are as equally sacred as you are, as holy as the breath of the Goddess by just being alive, should come as no surprise at this point.

Why Did You Write This Book?

To be as transparent as possible, this book is a collection of thoughts and exercises I've developed on my own or adapted from other sources over the course of many years of study. I've walked the path of the druid, studied under great teachers of witchcraft, and found a kindred spirit in heathenism. In my early childhood years, I held close and valuable connections with vari-

4. Eleanor Ainge Roy, "New Zealand river granted same legal rights as human being," *The Guardian*, March 16, 2017, https://www.theguardian.com/world/2017/mar/16/new-zealand-river-granted-same-legal-rights-as-human-being.

ous land spirits and would regularly talk to the birds that perched outside my window. I grew up in a very rural area and had a few friends, mostly spending my time immersed in books and in the experience and interaction with the magickal world.

My house was haunted, I saw UFOs fairly regularly, and was once chased by a large, dog-sized black cat. I was a latchkey kid, which meant I was responsible for my own care and maintenance much of the time. One time a car full of teenagers stopped in front of me and one of them pointed a long gun at my chest and pulled the trigger. There are no scars to prove that it happened and I came away with the feeling (even at the age of eight) that I had been *pulled* to an adjacent version of the universe where I had not been shot. Any and all of these are pretty good examples of what some describe as initiatory events into the unseen world. Tragic or just highly strange, events have a tendency to open one's psychic eyes and ears. I was destined for high strangeness ever after but attempted to cover it up or disregard it for years because it made me so different from my peers. By the time I was in my teens I started reading Church of Satan founder Anton LaVey's *Satanic Bible*, briefly dated a twenty-one-year-old Satanist who, no joke, appeared on one of those salacious talk shows where people air all their dirty laundry. However, I found the intrigue only went so deep and moved on from there to Buckland's big blue book. While that was also not a perfect fit, I found more of a kindred spirit in it, and it helped spark a love of the craft that would stay with me to this day.

At some point, I was initiated into a vampire coven that practiced a bastardized form of ceremonial magick complete with razors and bloodletting. It was a supremely strange part of my life that I rarely have spoken about since, but their magick was real and at times powerful. People like Michelle Belanger do it much better than the band of central Wisconsin misfits whose world I wandered through though. Some of them disappeared, ended up in prison, or were just so aghast at what they had created that they turned away and never came back.

After that, I burned a lot of bridges; it's easy to make mistakes when you're trying hard to excel at it. As I pushed further and further against my innate nature, and, in fact, against Nature toward what I believed to be a proper rationalist-materialist-science outlook, I became horrifically depressed. I had been married and divorced, put myself through college, narrowly avoided homelessness, and definitely did not avoid extreme food scarcity. For a summer, I lived almost entirely off of a large bag of almonds meted out in a small handful each day that someone had left at my house for a potluck. This also happened to be one of several times in my life I became very alcohol dependent. When the house is burning, why not add some gasoline, right? I somehow escaped college with an acceptable (though not stellar) GPA and ended up in Florida.

Now, the mere mention of the most notorious of US states has probably led you to quite a few assumptions about where this dumpster fire is heading, right? In fact, it turned around quite nicely. I met someone and we ended up being very complimentary, energetically. With life beginning to balance out, I returned to my spiritual exploration; rational-materialism had left me cold, and I wanted to pursue a more holistic life that included healing from the various knocks, dings, and soul-wounds I had picked up along the way.

As I started to work on healing, little bit by little bit, I began to realize that attempting to navigate the obstacle course of living in our culture was at best an accidental by-product of a system designed around extraction. At worst it was an intentional manipulation that was gas lighting most of the people who were forced to participate in it.

Whether it's accidental or intentional, the point is that it's happening. We are all losing bits of ourselves to the great beast. Cultural programming is an almost irresistible current that pushes you downstream even as you argue that a river shouldn't be here. Witchcraft can be a lot of things, and working magick through the craft can be done with a multitude of aims, but the reclaiming and healing journey is one of the most central pieces that allows you to truly evolve.

In certain schools of thought, to be a reactionary is about the most disempowered place one can be. If we live our lives always reacting to what's happening, we're not able to create a coherent path forward and out of the constant struggle.

By not reacting, especially when it's not absolutely necessary, we regain some power and control. If we want empowered magick, if we want spells that succeed and feel almost effortless, we first have to create boundaries. Physically, mentally, emotionally and psychically. It doesn't need to happen all at once, and being flexible is its own virtue, but start there.

Exercise
Setting Intentions

Get a notebook or a piece of paper and a pen: we're going to start the journey gently and simply. Think about the following question and start writing a list as things come to mind. Don't edit, just write, no matter what emotional response they bring up. Nothing is too big or small. Nothing is too petty or shameful.

> *Where is a place in which you have lost balance,*
> *where your boundaries are muddled or non-existent?*

Give yourself a couple of minutes. Most people, upon reflection, make a much longer list than they had anticipated. This is not a space for judgment. If you struggled to come up with anything, I'll just plop "social media" here as a freebie. If you don't use social media, bless you, you're one step closer to enlightenment.

The next step is a small bit of magick called intention setting. (If you're experienced with magick or yoga, you are likely already familiar with this.) Basically, we're going to say to ourselves and the universe itself that *these* are the new boundaries (whatever they may be). Grab another small piece of paper or an index card. Write down the thing that you intend to set boundaries with and then draw a firm and completely enclosed box around those words. Be gentle, pick something that's easier to accomplish first. For digital-only folk, you can write a new note on your phone and draw a box around it if that's what brings all the sabbatic goats to your yard (just don't complain to me if we have to end up burning it in ritual later).

Let's say you chose social media as an area in which you need to create boundaries. Draw that firm rectangle around those words and make sure the edges meet. This is psychological as much as it is magickal; they're pretty interrelated. Now, think of a boundary that you want to set. At the time I'm writing this, average social media use is 147 minutes per day, almost two and a half hours. You could set your intention around reducing that number or set an intention to not use Instagram or TikTok for a certain number of days or weeks. You want your boundary to be reasonable and achievable while still feeling like a challenge. Once you've figured out your objective, write it next to the box. Here's the important part: write it as if you've already achieved it, and try to avoid words that give it a negative spin. For example:

"I use social media less than sixty minutes per day."

"I use TikTok for ten minutes a day."

Now take a few deep breaths and let the oxygen give your brain a little heady feeling, and repeat the intention to yourself a few times until you feel as though it's settled within you. Take the paper and put it away somewhere safe. We'll pull it out again when it's time to work on new boundaries.

Some magickal workers believe that after the intention is set, it's important to put it out of your mind entirely. In the example of limiting social media, don't dwell on it or remind yourself about it every time you pick up your phone. Let the intention magick do the work that you set for it and move on.

Set a little reminder for yourself for a week from now (or if there was a time frame built into your intention, stick to that). When that time has concluded, reflect on what you accomplished during that time. Did you hit your goals? Journal about it and see how intention magick worked for you.

The social media example also lends itself to some pretty trackable metrics, as most phones have an app that shows you how much screen time you've had, broken down by application type.

Whether you accomplished your intentions or not, pull your list back out and pick another. Magick is as much about stepping into the animate flow of the universe as it is about experimenting to discover what works.

The Art of Destabilizing Your Cultural Programming

Setting intentions is a great first step for cracking open the window and beginning to smell the roses that bloom in the witch's garden. Accomplishing things that have seemed out of reach, breaking nagging habits, or even allowing yourself to rest can and should feel empowering. Accomplishments may also trigger the realization that you are doing important work, which can open up a can of worms. After all, if you're focusing intensely on something and then allowing it to evaporate into the ether, casting it away with the energy from your being, not allowing yourself to be concerned with the outcome and you're still having success that seems statistically improbable, isn't that sort of ... magickal? Most of the Western way of thinking casts this type of stuff as laughable, fringe, or simply not possible; the product of a deluded mind.

Letting go of that constant approval seeking might make you feel uneasy at first. Think about it: we go to school and must get good grades—no, *perfect* grades. We play sports and must be the most athletic, we must be attractive, a certain weight, have a pleasing temperament. If we have a hobby or a talent, we must sell what we create. When you start doing things for yourself because it's fun or you're passionate about it and don't seek approval, you may start to get some resistance from other people. But you're a strong, empowered person able to shake off the people trying to drag you down, right? Impervious to judgment? Ready to take on the world? Oh yeah, me too.

The truth of the matter is that when you start stepping out of line, everything becomes quite uncomfortable. People in communities fighting for respect and recognition are doubly familiar with this. Let's also consider for a moment that when you start speaking about things that don't add up for materialist rationalists, they get very angry. Generally speaking, I'm a big fan of the sciences. After all, the nature of curiosity drives scientists, just as it does witches, though I don't care for the tendency of witches, Pagans, and New Age-y people to bend theories to make them agree with things for which there is clearly no evidence, so let's not do that. Science is the pursuit of knowledge and is used to create theories about how and why things work. The true scientist knows that there aren't any conclusions, only theories that have likely outcomes. Nature, being infinitely variable, has a tendency to throw monkey wrenches into absolute declarations, which is where I see a lot of people who are fans of the sciences tripping themselves up. If you start talking about being able to affect yourself, the environment around you, or the outcomes of chance by using magick, you will likely make someone angry enough that they tell you're full of it. And maybe they're right some of the time, but they're not always right. Start digging into the world of quantum mechanics and you'll unearth a mountain of counterintuitive or even unbelievable behavior.

Breathe deeply and develop a thicker skin. One of the most compelling parts of becoming estranged from the current of thought that powers our society is that you suddenly start meeting a lot of other people like yourself. All you have to do is stop giving your awareness to the spectacle and turn around, we've been behind you all along.

2.
Fundamentals

There are a number of fundamental exercises that are necessary when doing the work of this path. They are shared widely and come in different flavors but boil down to some of the core work of modern witchcraft. These include grounding, shielding, maintaining a regular meditation routine, and clearing and cleansing your energy bodies, to name a few. There are countless books that run through these, and I encourage you to test out any you come across to discover what style works best for you.

If you are making your first hesitant footfalls on this exciting path, please read on and practice these techniques until you feel you have the hang of it. For the seasoned practitioner, you may choose to skip ahead if you like or try out some of these techniques if you've been away from them for a while to get a little refresher. They're frequently used, so it may be worth your while.

What's important is that you feel comfortable and confident with these methods because they're key to moving energy and making contact with spirits, all the while maintaining your safety and creating stable boundaries.

Grounding

The practice of grounding is exactly what it sounds like: a method to reconnect with your standard mode of operating; your state of mind and being when you're content, relaxed, and aware. Working in the spiritual realms can be taxing, and you may frequently find that once you've returned from your wanderings, your energy levels can be elevated, frazzled, or even leave you in a sort of stupor not unlike being under the influence of substances. Encountering certain deities or doing specific workings are notorious for the latter especially, but sometimes we have to do things like drive a car to get home after the ritual. Grounding is essential for returning unwanted energy and bringing it back into balance within ourselves.

Some of the most common ways to ground are to touch the ground with your hands or eat a small snack. Other methods I've used are stomping feet or moving hands in a sweeping motion over the body from the head down to the ground, gathering up the unwanted energy and depositing it into the earth. This method relies on the use of psychological signaling. Our subconscious mind will often react in a similar way to actions we do in real life as those done in pantomime. Have you ever had a dream that was just too real? One where you wake up and are confused that you're in bed because you were just talking to a close friend or jumping out of a building, superhero style? To your subconscious mind, it doesn't matter that you haven't physically done something in a dream, it's as if whatever happened actually happened. We'll access the same thing here but in reverse.

A great time to practice this exercise before you endeavor to do any spiritual work is when you're transitioning from one part of your day to the next. Coming home from work is a great time because you're frequently carrying so much of the day with you. Maybe you're grouchy or still hyped up from something exciting that you were working on and you need to make sure that isn't carrying over to your interactions with your partner, roommate, or family. Take a few moments away, remove your shoes, and plant your feet on the floor.

Exercise
Grounding

Close your eyes and breathe in slowly through your nose and gently release your breath out through your mouth. Do this for several cycles and begin to simply be present with your body. Think about how your body is your interface with the universe, how the universe has never experienced itself quite the way it has with your unique signature and assemblage of characteristics. Set aside your judgments and just offer a small amount of love and appreciation to your body for all it does. Give yourself a hug or a gentle caress if you feel inclined.

Now imagine that you're holding a stone at the area just above your head, sometimes referred to as your crown. Allow your consciousness to imbue the stone, filling it up so that you and the stone are one. When you are ready, let the stone drop to the ground and breathe out a puff of air as you do. On your rebounding inhale, pick the imagined stone up and place it in your pocket. Open your eyes and have a drink of water or a small amount of food.

Later in the book when we do journeywork, we'll come back to this exercise. When doing it, imagine placing all of the ungrounded, wild, or woozy energy you have into the stone before dropping it, helping to remove it.

Shielding

This practice is done by using your natural psychic energy to protect you from harm from another energetic source or being. There are a number of visualization tools you can use to help you practice but the basic one we'll use is that of a sphere of energy that encircles you. Think of it like a shell that is radiating around your body, impenetrable to unwanted forces, completely transparent. Anything that could potentially harm you will not enter. All positive energies can easily and cleanly pass through, like sunlight through a pane of glass.

Exercise
Shielding

To begin the practice of shielding, start with some deep breaths, drawing in more energy as you feel your power increase with each inhale and exhale. After a minute or so, draw your breath into your core, the center of your being, and feel a little sphere form. With each inhalation, expand the sphere more and more until you have filled it with radiant energy. Now, push one last time and feel the edges of the sphere that encircles you harden. Practice this exercise until it begins to feel like second nature, until you can execute the shield all in one breath. When you do so, you may start to put some conditions on the shield, allowing in energy that is healing while still filtering out energy being directed against you. As you develop your skills with these techniques, you'll develop an instinct of when to shield.

One form of advanced shielding is creating a wall or ward, which is a more permanent shield. Practitioners will often do this to create barriers around their homes, their cars, or anywhere else where they feel a more longterm solution is necessary.

Here's an anecdote as a warning about constructing these things that serves as a larger lesson about magick in general:

I once created a ward around my car; one of the conditions I had set was that my car would be unremarkable to police. But I made one crucial mistake: in the spell, I used the word "invisible." So when I was driving home one night after work and a county sheriff's car came across the center line and squarely smacked the side of my car, I immediately realized the mistake I had made.

After a quorum of officers from the city, county, and state—no less than fifteen—held court on the side of the road for an hour and a half, the verdict came back: Though I was clearly not at fault, I walked away with a ticket and a thousand dollars' worth of body work to boot.

Let my story be a warning: spellwork will always deliver. However, it might not deliver what you were expecting or hoping for, and sometimes you won't even see or perceive a result. All energy, magick included, has a tendency to follow the path of least resistance. If the parameters you've set don't account for all the variables or seek to mitigate negative outcomes, you may find yourself on the side of the road, cursing your invisible car.

Connecting the Above and the Below

The following meditation has many variations in the craft, which can also be used as an alternative way to the aforementioned grounding exercise. It's frequently used at the beginning of a ritual or other activity where energy will be raised and used in one form or another and I primarily use it to come into contact with the energetic force that animates the universe.

Exercise
Earth and Stellar
Darkness Meditation

Relax and get into a seated or standing position. Stretch your limbs, work out any kinks you feel in your body, stretch tight muscles and aching joints. Get some energy and blood flowing. Breathe deeply into your solar plexus, just below your heart and feel energy flowing in and out with each breath. When you feel full and perhaps a little light-headed, take another breath and send it down. Imagine a cord dropping from your root down into the soil. Send it deeper and deeper into the earth, through stone and underground rivers, through the mantle and straight into the molten core of the earth. Drink up that energy through your cord, pulling it up with each breath until the warmth enters your energetic body and spreads that warm feeling all around.

From that same place in your solar plexus, send up a cord of energy until it emerges out of your crown and let it reach far up into the sky, out of earth's atmosphere and beyond into the cold realm of the stars. Feel that stellar energy and breathe it down through your cord, down, down through your crown, feel that cold breath of space work its way through your chakras and meet the hot earth energy where they mix and churn together and begin spinning clockwise in your chest. Allow the radiance and magnificent feeling of this new energy work its way throughout your physical and etheric bodies. Know that you are now fully anchored not just to the earth but to the universe itself. Next, slowly release the cords to the earth below and the stars above. Keep the energy that you have pulled into yourself—don't let it go as the cords are released.

This is an exercise I do when I'm about to start a ritual or work some magick in one form or another, but I sometimes do it when I'm just feeling out of sorts or in need of a quick alignment. When working with really powerful energy, it can be especially noticeable when you have properly aligned yourself. I recall one time working with the Fae, I had not properly done this and came out of the work literally feeling like the room was spinning. I had to sit on the ground, the dizziness was so extreme. Doing the previously mentioned grounding exercise was helpful, but I felt out of sorts for the rest of that day until I was able to reset and restore with sleep.

3.

The Healing Journey

Magick, with or without the 'k', is one of the main reasons so many of us begin on this path. Witchcraft is fun, a lifestyle, a religion, a spirituality, a worldview, it can be none of those things or all of those things. But magick…magick is the thread that runs through so many different varieties and flavors of practice. Whether you practice seiðr, ceremonial magick, druidry, witchcraft, or some other garden variety Paganism, that essence of magick is what calls so many of us to this practice.

And why not? Magick holds the promise of agency in one's life, of being able to influence outcomes and make the miraculous real. As many practitioners will share, you become attuned to the patterns of life and are able to bend them when you start to work with magick for a long period of time. There are big and small acts of magick, from putting a dollar beneath a candle to landing a career opportunity to living exactly the life you had always wished for. And because we live in a highly interactive universe where people, spirits, gods, chthonic forces from other dimensions, blades of grass, and bad drivers are all exerting their own will, there tends to be a sliding scale of effort and probability on the small versus large acts of magick. As you'll read in other books, timing (i.e., using the astrological movements of planetary forces) and materials (stones, bones, herbs, spit, etc.) can be enormously helpful in turning outcomes in your favor. Some people use none of that and still manage impressive results. As with all things magickal, your mileage may vary.

One thing that becomes abundantly clear after you've been at this game for some time is that the more baggage you bring in, the more garbage comes out. In other words, if you come into your magick a salty, twice-baked witch, expect to have some salty, twice-baked results for whatever you're trying to accomplish. Your energy and attention matter for the end product. Let's do a little thought exercise on why that might be the case.

Say that you'd like to free up a little more time. You work a lot, you're tired, and you'd love to be able to focus more energy and attention on your craft. First, you try all the mundane ways you can think of to free up more time. Instead of streaming shows all night, you switch to just one. Instead of drinking a glass (or bottle) of wine, you make some tea. It's going to be a witchy night spent researching herbs and reading about the craft! But then you get tired and fall down the hole of doomscrolling on your preferred flavor of social media and before you know it, it's two in the morning, you're as parched as a mummy, and cursing yourself for a fool.

That first night was a bust. The next night, you try again, sitting down at your altar and making some strong declarations, but you're angry about something you've carried with you from work, and your relationship with your partner is starting to feel like your relationship with your parents. You write some stuff on a slip of paper, set it on fire, and then retire for the night. Maybe you write something like FOCUS or ENERGY, or maybe you've encountered metaphysical affirmations in your practice and write something like *"I have energy to achieve my goals."* Then you crash on the couch, and a month later, curse at the gods or the moon for a bit for not listening to your directives and making them a reality.

The thing is, you'll never be able to magickally make a flame move if you don't start working on yourself. It's the thing every witch hates to hear but to use a phrase frequently credited to Hippocrates, the ancient Greek father of medicine, "heal thyself." Especially if you intend to do workings for other people, the last thing they need are your trust issues with your mother coming through when they need a spell to sweeten their relationship with their boss.

Before we parade around cleansing and healing traumas, it's important for me to say that I'm not a mental health practitioner; seek help from a trained professional if that's what is appropriate for you. If at any point you believe this work is not right for you or that any of the workings or exercises triggers a response that doesn't sit right, set the book down and talk to a professional about what it brought up and how you can work to heal that part of yourself. You're better off not rushing your journey and giving it the time and space it deserves.

I admit, I'm not a picture of classical health. While much of what will be discussed ahead is about unraveling complexes in order to bring a greater sense of cleanliness to our work, lots of traumas get stored in the body. Our experiences with other humans, our jobs, generations of negative outcomes for our ancestors, systems created for profit and not people, not to mention the ogreish amount of social media we have consumed in its short lifespan affects how we look, how we feel about our bodies, and how our biology itself behaves. If you are a person obsessed with politics and consume hours of political content a day, consider what that might be doing for your overall well-being. Does your heart race every time you see a certain politician's face? Are you filled with disgust when said politician's supporters act in ways that feel incomprehensible, or that feel degrading and dehumanizing? Those emotional reactions affect your heart and influence hormones in your body.[5] Your stress response kicks in and you feel agitated and ready to do…something. Where do you even direct that energy? Social media is the response most people have but that just ends up starting the cycle over again.

Sedentary jobs have also changed the landscape of our physicality. According to the American Heart Association, sedentary jobs have increased by 83 percent since the 1950s and now make up 43 percent of all employment in the United States.[6] Americans spend a third of their lives working, a staggering number considering that also accounts for time off and childhood years. The full picture begins to unfold, of how we've gotten to a point where we have to make choices between adequate health and time spent working, running

---

5. "Stress effects on the body," American Psychological Association, November, 1, 2018, https://www.apa.org/topics/stress/body.

6. Allene L. Gremaud et al, "Gamifying Accelerometer Use Increases Physical Activity Levels of Sedentary Office Workers," *Journal of the American Heart Association* (July 2, 2018), https://doi.org/10.1161/JAHA.117.007735.

children around, pursuing advanced degrees we hope might pay off, having a social life (another thing that is intrinsically important to human health). Let's not even get into the demands of surviving a pandemic and environmental destruction, or how elected officials are actively conniving in every conceivable way to eliminate any programs that could a) benefit us or b) perhaps even recognize personhood or the ability to participate in a rapidly crumbling democracy. All of this, and that's a *good* day for many of us. I get it. And while I will never claim to know what it's like to walk in someone else's shoes, I have empathy for everyone who is struggling to get by.

Breath of Power

The breath of power is a little spell we cast on ourselves, not to alter or change anything, but to remind us of who and where we are. It's a gentle but affirming reminder that you are in your rightful place in the universe, as you always were.

When we breathe, we turn our attention to the body's autonomic processes (those that regulate heart rate, blood flow, sexual arousal, and respiration among others), which is tied to the sympathetic nervous system controlling our "fight or flight" response. Breathing like this is almost like manipulating the breath and is much easier to do than regulating the body's heartbeat or blood pressure. Think of it as a hack we can use to calm our body, ease our emotions, and quickly change our state of mind.[7]

Exercise
Breath of Power

This exercise can be done seated or standing, walking or running; the idea is that it's subtle enough that you can do it in public, even when face-to-face with someone (they will likely not pick up on what you're doing). If you can, vocalize the little charm that follows (it may help increase its power but is not necessary). Take one deep breath and then speak or think silently in your head:

---

7. Marc A. Russo, Danielle M. Santarelli, Dean O'Rourke, "The physiological effects of slow breathing in the healthy human," *Breathe* 13, issue 4 (2017): 298–309.

At home in my body,
At one with my souls,
Connected to the cosmos,
I remain whole.

While you're inhaling, empty your mind, attempt to settle into your most grounded state, and be as mentally unmoved as a mountain. Though the wind blows fiercely, you are unmoved in this moment.

Take another breath and repeat the charm. You are a mature redwood tree that has stood in the face of storms innumerable and remain unmoved.

Take a final breath of power and repeat the charm. You are the frozen tundra, unfazed by the howling winter. It is done.

Grounding with the Breath

The breath of power is a breathing technique where you engage a cleansing, empowering breath in order to reset or even settle into your power. Power can be a funny word for some that means a lot of different things. What you want to do here is feel as if you are empowered to do whatever it is you need. It's not a state of being more energetic, it's allowing your energies to deepen and expand so that you are able to stand with your being, not acting from a reactionary space.

Being reactionary is the very opposite of being powerful. Let's say someone says something you find to be hurtful. A reactionary response would be to counterattack and attempt to hurt them in return or worse, carry the grudge and do something truly foolish, such as trying to curse them. Meanness or cruelty are weapons, and they exist on the spectrum of aggressive action. Through the examples of our parents or those who raised us, our society has taught us that when we are hurt, we shouldn't accept what has been done to us and to seek retribution in some way. This mentality is one of the reasons our culture is so staggeringly and increasingly violent. When someone insults you, the feeling goes that they've taken something from you: your personal agency, your standing or respectability, and how others perceive you or how you perceive yourself. It feels unfair, especially in a system that is built around taking things from you and giving very little in return. It can feel like the last straw to be insulted by your friend or neighbor, or to be harassed by a stranger. In those exchanges, there's a power dynamic at play and by reacting negatively and engaging in the anger or passive aggression of your attacker, you in turn feed more power to them, further disempowering yourself.

During trying events, taking a moment to reset your mind and settle your soul and connection with your magick by taking a breath of power can help bring you back to a grounded state and reduce the likelihood of acting in a way you may later regret. If it's not possible in the moment to take a breath of power, just remove yourself from the situation and do it afterwards to restore yourself.

Exercise
The Heart Flame

Take some breaths as you did in the last exercise, and focus on your breathing. Then turn your attention to your heart space and imagine a flame illuminating it. A small candle burns there, always alight. If the flame or candle is a particular color, gently take note and keep your attention on it. Take a moment to notice the warmth of the flame spreading, radiating out through your body. Allow your muscles in your chest and torso to relax, allow your shoulders and neck to relax. Allow your hips, thighs, and down through your legs to relax. Now your arms become slack and begin to feel like they're gently resting on the earth. The muscles in your face and head finally relax, and every worry that you carry with you melts into the warm radiant energy from your heart space.

Give yourself this moment, rest your consciousness in the cradle of this experience, where your only concern is to allow the candle to keep radiating warmth through your being.

From within this deep, relaxing state, you will set an intention that whenever you need this feeling and for whatever amount of time, be it a moment or twenty minutes or more, all you need to do is take three deep breaths and call up the candle flame in your heart.

Now gently return yourself to wakefulness and alertness but keep this feeling of openness and acceptance with you as we move forward.

The Spiritual-Physical Connection

In the overlapping physical and metaphysical systems of the body are many systems that we should be aware of. Some, like chakras, energy (or etheric) bodies, and auras, you have probably heard about. If you haven't or would like to understand more about them and how they work, there is a list of resources at the back of this book to help you. Suffice it to say that just as there are systems that control and regulate biological processes, there are also energetic systems that control energetic processes in the metaphysical approach to the human body. These regulate different aspects of our energetic systems, and they can create problems when they're out of alignment, disrupting our psychic abilities and inhibiting our sense of connection to the universal energy of which all existence is a part. It's worth noting that I said "sense of connection" because the reality is that we are always connected with that universal energy. However, our ability to utilize or recognize it may be affected by blockages created throughout the process of living life.

When you go through life and experience heartache, loss, or aggressions from others, it can accumulate in your energetic self if you don't have a regular and effective routine for cleansing and clearing away the "psychic crud" that accumulates. In the worst cases where the effects are too catastrophic for you to healthily deal with, it can lead to walling off parts of your psyche. People who suffer from post-traumatic stress from witnessing or being a party to violence are very frequently victims of this, where the self is in some ways "shattered," leaving behind fragments of the self that need reintegration.

Soul Integration

Also called soul shards, these are the parts of yourself that have broken away; perhaps out of personal protection, you calved off that part of yourself in order to persevere. Victims of serious trauma may do this to simply stop the pain. Recognize your strength that has brought you here, but know that healing can only happen when you've reintegrated. Without reintegration, a piece of yourself could forever block you from moving forward. If you suspect that your soul(s) are not in a place of wholeness, it is extremely imperative that you work with a professional who can help you manage or heal from trauma. There are magickal techniques that can assist the process, but as with all magick, the more you work at a problem from multiple angles (including the tangible, physical world as well as the energetic), the more you increase your chances of overall success.

It's also important to recognize and understand when magick might not be the right tool for you. If you deal with issues related to paranoia, sustained dissociation, bipolar disorder, or schizophrenia (to name a few), it is imperative that you manage your diagnosis properly, speak openly with your mental health professional, and abide by whatever advice they give you. We want to be the healthiest, most empowered witches we can be, and sometimes that means recognizing that setting boundaries is needed.

Later in this chapter we'll begin some shadow work that may help to heal schisms that relate to the potential othering effects we sometimes carry guilt or shame around, but as always, it's best to seek guidance from your mental health practitioner. Soul integration happens when we have healed schisms or complexes and our souls are self-possessed and in full alignment. In my tradition, this alignment happens using the three-souls model.

Aligning Oneself

Aligning yourself is a very simple exercise that can make the difference between leaning out of your car window while giving someone a not-very-kind gesture and letting people's bad actions roll off you like water off a duck's back. Putting out bad energy can really alter how your day goes, so let's work on aligning ourselves for our own benefit and the benefit of others.

Most of the three-souls systems that have been adopted by modern witchcraft come from ancient texts, including the Torah. Typically there is a connection to a personal soul, something akin to the ego. Victor Anderson, Grandmaster of the Feri Tradition, referred to it as the Talker. We also have something like an animal, wild, or child soul, called Fetch, which resides in your root and can tie you to the land. Finally there is your godsoul, or Holy Daemon, which connects you to all of creation and represents the spark of the Divine within you. The system is a bit rudimentary; after all, if everything is divinity, if "the all that is" is simply part of the Star Goddess, how can they be evenly sliced up? It's also worth pointing out that in other systems there are an abundance of souls—five, seven, nine, or more. The three-souls theory is what I was taught, and it feels the most correct for me. Explore other ideas and systems and use what works best for you.

When doing this working, we'll be empowering each of our souls by breathing in the energy of the universe, paying special attention to each soul and then have one last clarifying breath at the end so they are all in alignment with one another. If you've never done this work before, fret not, we'll go through each step and make it all familiar by the end of the exercise.

Most of the exercises will start with you getting your body into a comfortable state. Go to the bathroom, have a drink of water, and find a place to sit where you can feel comfortable but attentive. We're not taking a nap, though when you finish some of these exercises, you may feel somewhat dreamy afterwards. If you have issues with chronic pain, get into a position where you feel most at ease—if that means a bolster, a chair, or whatever allows you to shift focus away from it, use it.

If you have experience with meditation, this will be easier but if not, no worries. As thoughts, preoccupations, song lyrics, et cetera arise, acknowledge them and assure yourself that you can come back to them later. This practice of acknowledgment and setting aside works very well for managing anxieties around work and other areas of life, too.

If you need help visualizing a safe place for what you've set aside, imagine them going into a neat little pile or a notebook. Don't spend too much time focused on them; set them down without judgment. Allow yourself to shift into a lower gear. If you are familiar with the different brainwave frequencies, we're aiming for an alpha state—relaxed but not in the deep meditation of theta. There are phone apps and Youtube videos that will play each of these different frequencies if you want to experiment with how they individually affect how you feel. You can even train yourself to "drop in" to the right state of consciousness when it's called for.

Exercise
Soul Alignment

Breathe and empty your mind of errant thoughts. Once you've gotten to a point where you feel relaxed but still fairly alert, scan through your body. Beginning in your fingertips, move your focus and attention around. What does it feel like to have your awareness there, to have your focus just in your fingertips? Gently move your focus to your hands and do the same thing: what is the world like from the viewpoint of your hands? Continue on to your wrists, arms, shoulders. Move down from the crown of your head, your neck, chest, abdomen, and upper and lower back. Continue the exercise through your groin, root, glutes, thighs, and hips, and on down through your knees, calves, ankles, feet, and toes. Take time with each area as you're scanning, and take notice of anything that seems out of balance before moving on. Send healing energy or just a warm, soothing feeling to any areas of pain or discomfort.

When you feel fairly comfortable occupying each of these areas, move your conscious awareness to your heart. Feel its gentle yet strong rhythmic beating. Now see that thumping create a spherical shape like a bubble about an inch around your heart. Feel that space connected to the greater cosmos, a part of you anchored in your flesh that after this life will return to the source of all that is. Take a deep breath and imagine the breath pulling up energy from deep within the earth and pulling down energy from the deep blackness of space. Feel these energies pouring through your body until they come to the energetic bubble around your heart. They rush to fill it in, and you feel a sense of ease and balance wash over you. Take some of that energy and breathe it up into the space right behind your forehead, the seat of the Talker. Feel it become awakened and cleansed. Now take some more and breathe it down into your root, where your Fetch is located, and feel it awakened and cleansed. Finally, send some energy above your head into your crown, where your Holy Daemon is located, breathing into it and awakening and cleansing it. When you do, feel a shower of stars rain down upon you, each soul that you have breathed into lines up within your body and opens up easier communication between the three. Allow your awareness to return to the present, and appreciate how this alignment has made you feel.

Etheric Cords

One of the most common things people deal with are etheric cords or threads, thin, wispy, almost spiderweb-like minuscule energetic lines that connect us to everyone and everything around us that we've come into contact with over the course of our lives. The idea is that these energetic cords will connect with people and places and remain there until they either fade away over time or initiative is taken to clean them up and disconnect potential drains on our own psychic energy.

Victor Anderson referred to them as aka threads, a term he likely picked up from Huna traditions.[8] He suggested working to clean them up and reclaim the energy that might needlessly be connected to, say, the kid you bought an ice cream cone from this afternoon. One explanation I particularly resonate with comes from *Evolutionary Witchcraft* by Thorn Coyle.[9] Thorn talks about the Sticky One, one of your souls (in Feri and many other witchcraft traditions, one of three) that is said to stick to everything, sometimes drawing in energy and in my experience, sometimes losing energy via the same means. The sticky one, or the fetch or fetchself, is the part of us rooted in our physical sex and associated with the root chakra. It is where we find our connections to our

---

8. Victor Anderson, *Etheric Anatomy: The Three Selves and Astral Travel* (Albany, CA: Acorn Press, 2004), 66.

9. T. Thorn Coyle, *Evolutionary Witchcraft* (New York: Tarcher/Penguin, 2005), 46.

animal nature, whose concern is the body's primal needs. In my own training, the fetch is best communicated with through the use of symbols as it doesn't respond to the use of words or verbal commands very often.

As you can imagine, the sticky nature of the fetch leads it to easily attach itself to everything around it. Regardless of distance or time, it can stay firmly attached to whatever it comes into contact with. I sometimes wonder about how these etheric threads may work differently for people who identify as introverted versus extroverted; I myself am particularly introverted and find simply interacting with a number of people exhausting until I have had a chance to rest and reclaim my energy from the experience. Extroverts, on the other hand, are energized by their experiences with others. Perhaps etheric threads represent a fundamental way of how we give and receive energy that splits between these two (or more) groups of people.

It's important for the sake of energetic cleanliness to be aware of and take opportunities to sweep up etheric threads and remove them from yourself at regular intervals. New moons are an excellent time to do so—think of them as lunar reset periods in which you can call back any energies to yourself and use them to set intentions for the new month. And if you can clear them out more frequently than the new moon, I encourage it.

Why Cleansing is Important

As someone who interacts psychically and magickally with the rest of the world, you have honed or are honing aspects of your innate being which interact with the world differently, or at least with more attunement, than a majority of people do. You've come in touch with what is essentially a muscle that most people have but haven't exercised and so they don't experience things the same way magickal and psychic practitioners do. Once your awareness is opened up and especially the more you utilize these unique skills your aura stands out like a bonfire on a dark night. All sorts of spirits that might like to feed off of your energy are attracted from far and wide.

Think of the work of the practitioner as flipping on a giant, bright neon light that says OPEN 24/7 and advertises the best pancakes in town. Late night diners would kill for the kind of pull we have. All the "little nasties" as

Christopher Penczak, founder of the Temple of Witchcraft calls them, are down for the pancakes we're serving up. Okay, I know I've stretched the metaphor to the breaking point now, but you get the point. It's important that we be cleansed, clear of any unnecessary energetic connections and shielded, to boot. If you're walking around with dozens or hundreds of etheric threads siphoning away energy or attaching you to people or things you wouldn't give your ZIP code to, let alone your phone number, it can be a challenge to keep those shields up.

It is rarely mentioned that etheric cords run both ways. Pity the witch who has started dropping hexes and didn't keep themselves energetically clean and free of etheric threads, because that's the first place to look when you suspect someone might be giving you the business. Tracing those cords is a simple task for someone who knows what they're doing, and they might just be happy to send a little jolt along that path for your effort, too.

Exercise
Clearing Away Etheric Cords

Let's get rid of any extraneous ties and reclaim some of our power in the process. In following exercise, I've included a couple of methods to clear away etheric cords. While there are many other ways to do this work, too, these are two great basics to have in your toolbox.

Start by grounding and centering yourself by performing the earth and stellar darkness meditation.

1. Cutting etheric cords

When you feel settled and sufficiently anchored, expand your awareness outwards. Do the heart flame meditation from earlier and follow the radiating warmth out. Feel the warmth spread from your chest in pulsing waves, awakening your belly, neck, your root, arms, legs, fingers, toes, and out through the crown of your head. Feel the energy gently come into contact with your fetch self. It forms a bubble a few inches off of your body all around you. There's an energetic buoyancy you'll become familiar with the more you work with it; there's an almost tactile bounce you'll notice when you come up against it. Take a few moments to familiarize yourself with it, energetically scan it, "see" with your mind's eye how it sort of follows the form and contours of your physical body. Now begin "feeling" all around it. Take your time and go over it carefully and feel for spots that seem weak. As you work, threads will become apparent, a bit like how objects at night become more visible the longer you allow your eyes to adjust. It may sound odd, but you can imagine the newly formed buds or eyes on a potato as a visualized and imaginal feeling of what you're scanning for.

As you find a cord, you can pull on it; sometimes it becomes quite clear to whom or what that cord is attached. Most of the time, it's something benign: a book you picked up in a store, your partner, someone you shook hands with at work, even a magickal working you've done that's still unfolding. It's important to remember that in the wrong hands, those connections are important paths that lead directly back to you, so we're going to work to assess them and cut them all (maybe not the spell unless it's outlived its usefulness). Generally, I like to use my athame for this task because it's quick and clean. If you don't use one, that's fine; a witch's finger can cut sharp as a knife when called upon. When you've figured out which cords need to be cut, take up your athame or pointed finger and sweep through them, one by one. As you do, say something to the effect of:

I cut you now and call back to me, you errant cords of energy,
I reclaim what's mine and return to whole, empowering myself and
my three souls. So mote it be.

Afterward, you can set down the athame (if using) and scan your etheric body again to see if you missed anything. Using a magickal tool will generally do the trick and leave you with a pleasantly whole and self-possessed feeling that can be quite surprising if you haven't done it in a while.

2. Resetting your energetic state

Sometimes you just need a reset. This can be useful when you've had too many irons in the fire for too long or if you just want a fresh start. This version of the exercise will eliminate all of the cords you've got sticking around, including any ongoing spellwork that you've stayed connected with, so be warned!

Take some deep breaths and center yourself. If you feel the need to use your athame to focus your intent, you may, but we won't be using it to cut anything this time. Much like the previous exercise, we're going to work from our Heart Flame, pulling in energy from the sky above and the earth below, expanding and filling the etheric fetch self with as much energy as possible. That said, don't overdo it—if you feel as though you've taken too much in, release some. The point you want to get to is that "full" feeling where you're pressing out against your etheric body. As in the last exercise, you'll feel etheric cords tracing off in different directions. This time, however, don't focus on them—just focus on grounding yourself.

Let the energy swell suddenly and see it pop, dropping all cords and attachments. Say out loud:

I call back all energy that is rightly mine, a spool of thread, reset,
rewinds; empowered now and self-possessed, I return to wholeness
and by the universe, blessed. So mote it be.

Don't be sentimental—you're not permanently severing your connection with loved ones or anything like that; they'll still put up with you as much as they did before, I promise. If you have concerns about cutting these cords, think of it like hanging up the phone at the end of a conversation. You wouldn't just leave the phone on and put it back in your pocket. You hit the red button and move on with your day. The connections you have with loved ones go deeper than these etheric cords, so don't be afraid to press the red button so you can both get on with your lives.

I try to do this type of cord-cutting more frequently than once a month. If you're someone who has to work with the general public, it can't hurt to make it part of your regular routine. Do it regularly and it becomes a part of psychic hygiene (especially if you have a social job), as important as bathing and putting on clean clothes. You wouldn't wait tables with the same shirt that had wine spilled on it yesterday (I hope!), it's the same thing for this sort of work.

Deactivating Lost Spells

One thing I'd like to circle back to is the bit about current workings. Based on your demeanor and experience with the craft, you may find that you do a lot of spellwork or rituals for different things. If you've created a handful of workings that require ongoing input, e.g., a spell that works as a furnace to keep energy flowing toward the continued success of something, you may occasionally forget one—a talisman that has gone unfed for too long, a spirit house you've set aside because the pressing need behind its creation subsides. It's important to track these things down and properly deactivate them when the time comes. Also recognize that the second working I've created above is sort of a master reset for *all* energy. It includes things that you want to keep working, so be aware. It might be worth your time and effort to meditate and identify the things that you're connected to that you no longer want, rather than tossing out everything you're working on and having to set it up all over again.

Demons

Everyone's favorite squirm-inducing topic is demons! There was a comic panel that circulated on social media for a while where someone was attempting to summon a demon but the spell was written in cursive and the character accidentally summoned a lemon instead. That sort of mistaken identity is a good starting point when we talk about demons. We're not working with the goetia here—these are your personal foibles, darknesses, shames, or your shadow. And as much as you other it, your shadow is still yours.

Unlike goetia, which can be summoned as servitor spirits (or drive you mad if you don't know what you're doing), your shadow "demons" are always with you. Unlike your Holy Guardian Angel, they aren't your direct, personal contact with divinity but working with them can lead you that way.

As I've mentioned with several other healing practices here, we're brushing the surface of a well that has no bottom. You can and should continue a regular practice with all of these things throughout your life. There are a countless number of books on the subject from many religious backgrounds and from no religious background at all, in the case of working with complexes, for example. Most of it will not resonate with you because it just won't speak to you, it won't work within your spiritual framework, or it's just Tuesday and try as you might, you're just more naturally combative and Aries-like on Tuesdays. That's okay. Here's one way I've found some success with that seems to fit within the general framework of witchcraft. It may also be more useful for people who have spent time with a professional mental health practitioner to be able to identify the roots of your issues. Again, I am not nor do I make claims to be a licensed mental health counselor or medical doctor. If you read this and find information that is useful and beneficial, awesome.

Understanding the Shadow

First, let's get some terms out of the way: what we'll be looking at is what is typically called the shadow or shadow self. It's not a detective from a 1930s radio drama—as mentioned above, it is the unacknowledged parts of yourself. For some, it's the parts that they haven't ever even thought about. Not everyone navel gazes quite as thoroughly as I do, I've come to realize, and perhaps I need to do less of it! But what it has brought to light are the many complexes that underpin my personality and the reasons I behave and react as I do. Some of it has seeped into what I would call core identity and complexes that are very hard or impossible to uproot.

It was a distressing to find things that were so distasteful, lodged so deeply in myself. But this is what happens when we work with our shadows, we find layers upon layers of history that have, in essence, metastasized around something. When we work with our shadows, we find layers upon layers of history that have, in essence, metastasized around something. The first step is to bring them out into the open and acknowledge them. What created this fear, this anxiety, this anger?

I'll lead by example, by airing dirty laundry. I have a deeply ingrained rejection of authority. I carry it with me still, and over the years it's been a dangerous influence that has landed me in some very precarious situations. But after learning about, acknowledging, and finding the root (or in lots of cases, many roots) of the issue, I have turned it into a powerful ally in advocating for myself and others. It's helped me say *no* in no uncertain terms to those who would use their authority to abuse me or my friends. It's turned into a potent battery for magick in the service of others in pursuit of justice.

How did I discover that this was a problem so that I could turn it into an ally? I noticed that I would frequently butt heads with people—and not just anyone, but bosses or even executive leadership, cops, bureaucratic functionaries—basically anyone who held power in some way over me or who could use their power to take mine away. Cops and politicians were the worst and continue to be the ones who push my buttons the most, but any paper Napoleon will do.

Even now, after working with my shadows around this, I still have interactions with some of these folks that could be best described as tense or confrontational. The difference is that I'm aware of what I'm doing and working with that characteristic rather than handing my power over to an unexamined and dangerous-for-me demon.

What's at that root? Where did this thing start to form? It's complex, but a little of my history: I was raised by very young parents and exposed to a lot of their very young friends when I was a child. At the age I'm at now, I think they were still children when they had children, even though they were technically adults. Several things happened over a number of years that turned me from a very trusting child to a very cautious one. In the interest of self-preservation, I had to learn how to protect myself and, as it correlated to my circumstances, that meant a blanket suspicion on authority and its motives. On the surface, I was a "good kid"—never suspended from school, detention only once or twice but mostly because I had learned to operate off the radar of adults. In my twenties, I got more in people's faces about things, which is when I started imagining there must be a better way. Finding the one or several inciting incidents at the heart of it was essential, though, because it allowed me to unwind the pain or trauma and rework it.

And that's magick.

It's such deeply transformative magick that it shouldn't be occulted; it should be a rite of passage to be able to pull these things out and heal them as best we can. We don't live in that kind of world, generally speaking, but witchcraft can provide one. We can't unmake things, but we can unlearn the patterns of behavior that make our traumas an active presence in our daily lives.

My Journey as a Point of Relation

Because I'm a person who needs examples of things that seem a little esoteric, here's an example of how I actualized this work of healing in my own life.

I've spent a large portion of my life being painfully introverted and feeling just alienated from others. This was in no small part due to my upbringing as a Midwesterner (especially my family), where the proper way to for children to be around others was to be quiet and not interfere with the adults. This upbringing led me to become a distanced adult who was cold and relatively impersonal. But underneath it all, I was a sensuous Taurus with a Pisces moon. I was a dreamer, a lover, a poet flooded with emotions and programmed to deny all of it. It was a recipe for disaster that led to many disastrous relationships and friendships. Like many in our culture, I was emotionally stunted and couldn't even allow myself to feel my feelings, let alone share them with others—I didn't know how. The harder I tried to push through the blockages, the more of a pariah I became; I had no models for how to push through other than being brash, aggressive, or consumed by my own wallowing despair and crushing depression.

I recall going to parties and just standing around, not really talking. Sometimes I offered to help but still felt like I shouldn't even be there. When a relationship soured, my ex told me they didn't know how to help me anymore, and there wasn't anything more to say. Granted I was navigating a world of damaged people, but I was shying away from my own personal responsibility for my share of the mess. These are red flags, but if you're in that sort of constant miasma of unknowing, it's challenging to unravel anything and have it make sense. More than once, I wished I could hit some sort of cosmic reset button to give me another chance to start over.

The issue was that I was trying to navigate my adult world with the broken tools I had been given in childhood. Raised by people who were little more than children themselves, the tools interacting with others I received were far from adequate. One of my demons became the isolated victim. Looking around our culture now, it's rampant, especially with young men. Isolated victims are hurt individuals, but they also carry that hurt as an unuseful and dangerous identity. They may feel like freedom fighters, attempting to rebalance the scales of perceived injustice through whatever cultural lens they have.

The first step toward acceptance was unraveling the narrative of the isolated victim and listening to that avatar who had been created within. And first, it meant identifying who it was.

I had the good fortune of having been in a relationship with someone who was on her own healing journey and her example led me to a deeper conviction of my own healing potential. Journaling and meditation were also helpful in the work of processing because they gave me the gift of extra perception. When you go back and read through journals, they can help jog your memory or help you see things afterwards that weren't clear while you were writing them. I kept daily journals for years and years that helped me understand some things about myself. First, I was dealing with an enormous amount of hurt. It started to become clear that wherever I went in life, I was experiencing this hurt, it wasn't improving, and the more life experience I had, the more hurts accumulated. Second, I was not equipped with the right emotional tools to address my needs. Repeatedly I saw myself trying to address my problems, but no matter how hard a person tries, a meal can't be cooked if there isn't a fire. In meditation, I would summon this angry, sad person and ask them what it was they needed, what they were actually after that would make them whole and turn them into an ally so we could move forward as a single person. At first, the answer was simply love. This part of me that felt like it was rejecting love in every action just needed to know it was loved. So I gave that part of myself love. I would look at myself in the mirror and say, "I love you. Even if you feel like no one else does, I love you."

It took a very long time for things to settle in, but eventually I got to a point in meditation when I asked, "what do you need?" and that other side, that demon, said, "understanding." And so I gave it my understanding, taking it to mean providing tools that would open that part of myself to greater understanding. I started reading about methods of communication, what healthy communication looks like, and methods for resolving conflict. I learned that I grew up with a deeply passive-aggressive communication style that I recoiled from, but I had no other examples. As a result, I was stand-offish so that I wouldn't suffer after emotionally investing. I feared being manipulated by others' attempts to make me feel guilty for not seeing things their way, so I would stay vigilant around anyone new. I took those tools to my shadow self, worked on them, and built trust and slowly built up a degree of confidence that I hadn't had before. Finally, I knew it was time to reintegrate this part of myself that I had been working with as an "other" so that I could attain a sense of wholeness and healing again.

Ritually, I encountered myself, the shadow I had been carrying with me for so long, whom I had fought against and felt shame for carrying and I now saw as a close ally who had been essential to my process of healing and wholeness. In the candlelit darkness of my altar, I asked it to rejoin me while looking at my reflection in a black mirror. From that moment, the two were made one again. Stronger than before, I was happily standing in my true identity that I had been struggling to find all along.

Exercise
Reintegrating the Shadow

Now we'll go through a number of small exercises to begin the process of reintegration of our shadow, the demons that plague us and prevent us from being the strong, powerful and balanced witch we were meant to be. This is a multi-part exercise that you should take your time with. At certain points I give suggestions on the number of times you should work on a particular spot, but take as long as you need and go at your own pace.

1. At the gateway

We begin as always, with some nice even breaths. As we do, we gently put away all errant thoughts and focus simply on breathing. Do this until you've achieved a sense of calmness and resolve. You should feel slightly detached from the world but in a light and buoyant way. Turn the corners of your mouth slightly upward to a very subtle smile. You have the power to change things and know that it can feel effortless, with practice and patience. Now walk yourself through the alignment and earth and stellar darkness meditation exercises mentioned earlier. Once you have connected to the earth and stars, to the great below and the great above, find yourself now at the base of a tree. Search along the base where the roots have curled to make a large pool. Gently enter the pool and feel the cool water, its touch quenching something deep within you. Instinctively, you know that you must dive into the water, into the darkness of the pool. If you choose to do so, you find yourself absorbed into the inky shadows and become disoriented for a moment. Down begins to feel like up, but before you have time to think or worry about it, you break through the surface of the water. You find yourself in a subterranean chamber, a cave that feels at once foreign and familiar. The cave appears to extend onward and downward, turning a bend just out of sight. As you walk along, you find the cave walls to be lit with a sort of blue bioluminescence. It seems to be virtually impregnating all the rock walls and allows you to safely traverse the space. Up ahead, you see the shadowy outline of a figure. As you approach, you see that their arms are crossed and they seem set on turning you away. They seem familiar but you don't think you've ever met them before. You get the impression that they're trying to block entrance for what they believe is your own safety. What do they look like, this guardian? What do they represent to you? Be present with them and ask them questions if you like. They seem stern but caring, not intimidating or frightening in any way.

You begin to understand that with the right gift, you may be able to persuade them. What gift or offering do you have that could sway this guardian of your deeper self in your favor? It could be energy, a promise to bring back something they like, or a promise to yourself. Sometimes spirits need us to manage tasks that are difficult or impossible for them to achieve in the material world. If you're able to give them a satisfactory offering, you see them uncross their arms and step aside. If you choose to move forward, you see a light ahead and then enter a room illuminated by torchlight. Inside are two benches across from each other. On the walls are broken shards of mirror of countless colors. If you take a moment to look at the pieces of mirror, you see memories from your life reflected in them, some good, some bad, but mostly just seemingly random bits. Some are shadows of memories, things that are unclear or fuzzy, things that you're unsure of. Also mixed in are what you know are false memories but all of these exist in a sort of simultaneous universe of your personal experience.

After a few moments looking, you feel compelled to sit on one of the benches. If you do, you are immediately confronted with a mirror image of yourself. It's a perfect reflection, copying exactly how you move, talk, and breathe, but you notice that there's a sort of haze around it, a fuzziness that makes it seem a little ethereal.

"What are you here to heal?" it asks before returning to a perfect mimic of you again.

Your memories are all around you, but you know there's something in particular that's been plaguing you that you want to move through and heal in order to move forward. Sit in contemplation with yourself: it could be irrational anger, a desire to use people, an addiction, or another unhealthy behavior. If you can't put your finger on it today, you can thank your reflection for its time and come back another day after you've thought about it. If you have something, you may proceed.

2. Ask yourself

Tell your reflection what you need help with. What do you believe were the inciting incidents that created the problem you're dealing with? While you speak, your reflection takes on more and more of the characteristics you describe—whether it's sadness, anxiousness, anger, or whatever else, you see yourself acting in those ways reflected back to you.

Remember: this is a reflection of an aspect of yourself. In this setting, it cannot harm you.

What would it look like for you not to be troubled with this issue? Talk to yourself and ask yourself questions. What does this other you need? How can you bring it back into yourself and heal the rift? Could a deepening understanding of why you react the ways you do begin to make changes? Listen carefully to the answers and see what thoughts and emotions it brings up in you.

At this stage, we're seeking, searching for information; there are no right or wrong answers. After this initial meeting, take a break and return here later. Journal each experience you have and read through them regularly to see what sort of themes arise.

3. Give

After you've done the above exercise a few times and are starting to uncover and reveal things to yourself, it's time to start giving your reflection, your shadow, this demon-like part of yourself what it needs. You may think, "oh, that's a terrible idea! It wants to ruin me or others." However, this is where you need to analyze what you're looking at and the information you're receiving. Dig a bit deeper and you'll see that validation, recognition, or love might be what's needed.

When you carry a burning ember of anger everywhere, could it not be from a deeper sense of disempowerment, personal or cultural? If the world looks like a dumpster fire (believe me, I know this one) and it makes you sick with sadness, sending acknowledgment and recognition of the problem while also giving examples of things that seem to be better might be in order. Sometimes simply listening to your shadow is all that it needs to unlock or unbind knotted up energy. What I've provided here are examples—only in working with your complexes as they are reflected to you can you begin to gain awareness of how *you* can heal. And remember that talking to a mental health professional about what you uncover is never a bad thing. It is especially important to work with a professional if you uncover deeply repressed issues that are alarming.

After working with your shadow and giving it what it needs for a while, see how it reacts to you when you do this exercise. Note any changes in your own view or outlook of the world regarding this particular issue.

4. Ally and reintegrate

The next and final active stage is to take this part of your shadow and reintegrate it within yourself. By turning the wheels of personal acceptance inward, you begin to gain acceptance of yourself and understanding of things about who you are that have made you uncomfortable. Reintegration is an important final step to returning yourself to a sense of wholeness. Only from a feeling of wholeness can you really begin to have healthy relationships and utilize your full power as a witch.

Ritual is the best setting for completing the reintegration process as it helps you process on several levels. While we haven't ventured too much into the ritual elements of our practice yet, you will have an idea of different practices you can do if you're familiar with other practices. If not, we'll work on an exercise you can use here.

It's best to do this at night or in a fairly dark room; the effect isn't quite the same in a well-lit space. Gather together a candle, a lighter or matches, and a mirror or reflective surface. It's better to have something you can prop up to gaze into easily, but you can use a bowl of water to gaze into if necessity calls for it. Just be sure that you'll be able to see your reflection.

Get comfortable in your space and set up the candle on a table or bench, somewhere safe where it won't get knocked over. Set up the mirror or whatever you're using and dim the lights.

After you've got everything set up to your liking, sit down and get comfortable. Take some deep and even breaths and really get into a relaxed state. Do the candle exercise from earlier in the chapter, imagining the candle light illuminating outward from your heart space and filling you with warm, healing energy. As it radiates outward begin thinking about your shadow self, your dark twin whom you have allied with and experienced in your healing journey. Call to them by whatever means seem appropriate, or use the following chant:

> *Dark self, shadow being,*
> *Demon and Other*
> *Come now in healing*
> *To join the two together*

Now stare into the mirror and gaze into your reflection. Recall the journey you've taken to get to this point, working from seeing this part of yourself as an adversary, a source of shame, or something you simply never acknowledged and pushed away. Recall the work that went into beginning to understand where this shadow arose from and what it felt like to open yourself up to compassion and give this part of you the love it needed rather than treating it like a problem or something shameful.

Stare into your own eyes and now, simply see yourself. Know that this reflection is no longer a shadow but part of your own being. You are one, whole—not a splintered person, not shards of personality who work at odds with one another—a whole person who takes responsibility for their past and ownership for themselves, and who has integrated completely.

When you look in the mirror, look at yourself with love. Look at yourself with the knowledge that you've achieved something tremendous that few people do or have the courage to face within themselves. Feel gratitude toward yourself for the effort you had to make and the uncomfortable and fierce honesty it took to get here. You've made yourself a more powerful witch and a more whole human by doing so.

As we wind down our ritual, give a little gratitude out to the universe, fueling it through the candle in your heart space. A simple message of thanks or a feeling of love sent out before you blow out the candle in your ritual space will suffice. Take a few deep breaths and bring yourself back to normal awareness. Have some food or water, and journal your thoughts about your experience.

There's no set amount of time you should take to rest but it is an important final step.

Just as being othered by society has led to a schism, othering parts of yourself leads to schisms and sometimes potentially dangerous mental health disorders. Owning where you have been and the healing journey that you took are the most important steps now. You are a whole and actualized human being and have grown through this process. By making the effort to heal, you have proven to yourself that you're worth it, which is fundamental to stepping into your witch power.

Compassion and Empathy

This work is fairly endless, as you may have gleaned. Just because you've gone through one cycle of reintegrating shadow parts of yourself doesn't mean there aren't others that also need care and attention. The real secret to this work is that it always continues. Becoming a person in alignment can be considered a journey and not a destination. Living beings are fallible, and the greatest example of that fact is seeing what happens to our infallible gurus and spiritual leaders who suddenly find themselves embroiled in scandals of their own making. Many are or were great humans, exploding with compassion and love, but the process of growth and personal work never ends, in my opinion, as long as you are enfleshed. Sometimes people fall into the belief that they have arrived at a destination when the road still continues ahead and out of sight. There are a lot of reasons why this may be the case but, ultimately, it comes down to the fact that we live in a complicated world.

It's therefore important to cultivate or deepen our own empathy and compassion. To some people, it might not feel like the most "witchy" thing but as we've discovered, this path is about healing as much as it's about casting spells. It's about deepening integrity as much as it is about casting astrological charts. Empathy may not be immediately satisfying, but it opens you up to the ebbs and flows of energy and gives you a greater understanding of patterning in human life.

An example: while writing this book, someone took great pains to make a project I was working on seem like something it wasn't. It took on all the character and color of how disagreements play out these days: they went to social media, started spreading rumors, made fake accounts to make it seem like the chorus of voices was louder than it was, and spread disingenuous (and in some cases, outright falsehoods) about what had happened. They were on a crusade over what was in reality a very small disagreement. My initial thought was to react with righteous indignation—honestly, who were they to smear something I had worked so hard on? What gave them the right to lie about me and others? I was angry, and rightly so. But I took some time to reflect on my anger and attempt to understand their point of view. To be frank, they were just someone who was attacking something very small for problems that were enormous and systemic. I realized they were fighting imaginary enemies in order to make themself feel in control and foster the belief that their efforts were having a net good effect. Their targeting was a real mess, though. So I wrote a message thanking them for reaching out and for the intent of their message, politely adding that it's a good idea that we no longer associate.

This person's problems were clearly not mine, and I was not about to take them on. But rather than engaging them and starting a witch war, the compassionate thing from my perspective was to simply not give them the oxygen they needed. While working with your own shadow is a process of listening, feeding, and coming together, the work of community is sometimes about drawing boundaries. As I began to understand what this person needed, I knew I could never provide it for them, nor was there anything I could supply that would right the ship for them. They were in love with their sense of martyrdom and righteous indignation. In those circumstances, it's a trap that only they can help themselves out of, and that freedom can only come from deepening self-knowledge and improvement or the love of friends or family committed to waking them up. Most of us will go through these phases, sometimes more than once.

Remember, as you deepen compassion for yourself, try to do so for others in equal measure. Compassionate people are world changers, even if they only touch the lives of the people around them at their jobs or in their neighborhoods.

Sometimes the best tools on a spiritual path are questions. Questions give us an opportunity to discover more about ourselves, who we are and who we would like to be. Consider meditating on the following questions and see what answers arise. Sit with them for periods of time and listen for how your immediate reactions may shift, as you move from reaction to compassion. Especially pay attention to quick and heated emotions like anger or cold and stagnant emotional reactions like feelings of powerlessness. See if spending an extended period of time sitting with each helps shift how you feel.

- How does a person live authentically in this world? Am I in touch with my own authenticity?
- How do people react when they're fearful? Is living without fear possible?
- When I disagree with someone, what physical reactions are triggered in my body? Does that physical response prevent dialogue?
- In general, do I feel safe and what action would make me feel safer? How can I help others feel safe around me?
- Are my needs and desires something that I take seriously?
- Am I a biased person? How do my biases help me "other" other people?

Remember that there aren't any right or wrong answers. The point of the activity is to bring awareness to your personal responses and then use those to help you understand how others respond when they feel fearful, unsafe, or unrecognized.

4.

Art and Magick

Throughout this book, I'll ask you to work on projects as a vital part of the process of integration and knowing. The way we will do this is through the language of the lower soul, the animal instinct or fetch as it's called. Your fetch and godsoul have an intimate form of communication that your middle soul, or talker, doesn't have. That's why when we're empowering our three souls we work from the talker to the fetch and up to the godsoul or holy daemon. Talker is too, well, talky... too rooted in the world of reasoning and logic to be able to adequately communicate to the godsoul directly, so it must mediate through the fetch, who is master of symbolic thinking and symbolic communication.

Think of talker as the part of you who's constantly checking your phone, distracted, chatty, and full of self-importance. When you silence the primacy of the ego, you give room for fetch to stretch and express in ways that are dynamic, therapeutic, even. And how does Fetch express itself? Through art, of course.

Some of you may be groaning right now—"Seriously? Art? We have to do art projects as part of this work?" And my answer is, yes, absolutely you do, it's a vital part of the process and one of the core parts of being human. We would be a very different species without art. If you're feeling trepidation, just know that "art" is a very broad term that includes traditional concepts that might involve brushes, paints, pencils, or canvas as well as motion, music, dance, performance, poetry, and other forms of mythopoetic writing. And yes, "art" also includes knitting, sewing, and crafting—y'all are part of the club, too!

As fundamental as art is to defining humanity, magick has always been with us, too. And there are some who would say that they're simply the same thing. Famous comic book creator and magician Alan Moore, known for work on such graphic novels and comic books as *V for Vendetta, Swamp Thing, Batman: The Killing Joke,* and of course, *Watchmen,* believes that magic and art are synonymous: "Magic in its earliest form is often referred to as 'the art.' I believe that this is completely literal. I believe that magic is art and that art—whether it be writing, music, sculpture, or any other form—is literally magic."[10]

For the purposes of this book, "art" is anything that allows you to disconnect from the logical world and get into a flow state. Flow states are defined as feeling mental readiness and alertness while being deeply involved in a task that generates either excitement or enjoyment in a person. You're absorbed in what you're doing but don't feel as though you're exerting any energy. It's as if you've plugged into some universal well of positive creative energy that allows you to keep working on a task without distraction or anxiety, almost as if you've escaped from time itself. The term was coined in 1975 by psychologist Mihály Csíkszentmihályia.[11] With his team, Csíkszentmihályi studied artists who got so absorbed in their work that they disregarded or simply forgot about normal biological needs such as food or sleep. In interviews with the artists, watery description words kept appearing, such as "being in the flow," or "I was floating." The team followed that lead and named it a "flow state."

Water is an interesting element for artists to work with. If you're not someone who has practiced any artform before, it might come as a surprise— you'd think maybe the air of the mind or the fire of the will (especially the creative potential held within fire) would be better fits. We are trained and taught to think of water as the realm of the feminine and emotions—while that's true, water is also a powerful storehouse of creative energy. Consider-

---

10. DeZ Vylenz, dir., *The Mindscape of Alan Moore* (Shadowsnake Films, 2003), DVD.

11. Mihály Csíkszentmihályi, *FLOW: The Psychology of Optimal Experience* (New York: Harper & Row, 1990), 40.

ing the generation of life created in the primordial seas, we can understand water's chthonic and underworld associations. Because we all must go there when our living bodies expire, our collective journey through the underworld brings us through the generative cycle of rebirth. In the same way, our art goes deep within our own beings but is also able to go deep within the collective consciousness, into the underworld of the universe where we may discover and retrieve beautiful gems of wisdom and power.

In the twenty-first century, art is many things but most frequently escapes the grasp of the common person. Art, as in what we see hanging in museums, is thoroughly commoditized and is seen as a way for wealthy people to amass even more wealth through investments. The cultural value that pieces of art have (or used to have) has begun to buckle under the weight of commodity. NFTs are one bastard brainchild of this philosophy and really expose how lost our culture has become: their creators saw the ballooning art market and its scarcity and used both as a model for creating a monetary system that revolves around digital goods. Now we're in the distasteful and regrettable situation of alleged adults discussing things like nyancats and how one man claims to own the original nyancat of which all other nyancats are derivatives because he paid money for it—hoarded wealth is the only thing of value in our culture.

Why Make Art?

The earliest representations of art are from caves, almost unimaginably ancient paintings set down by our ancestors. It would be easy to miss the simple fact that many of us likely have common ancestry connecting us with the people who put their work on those walls. But we really do—if not directly, then through the shared cultural heritage found in those ancient caves.

Today, it's almost a cliché to discuss the caves at Lascaux, though in recent years potentially older examples of cave art have been found. Lascaux has been mentioned so frequently in news and television shows that it's an inescapable cultural object that ironically few people fully understand. To our modern minds, we hear "cave art" and think cavemen, who, thanks to some early bad science and pop culture, became the epitome of the crude, unthinking dullard smashing rocks together and senselessly assaulting their compatriots. What needs to be remembered about these people—if there are any assumptions we can make about a people who lived so incredibly long ago—is the bravery and spark of divinity in creating paints that have lasted scores of millennia and the attempt to use figurative expression to capture what their world was like and what it meant to them. While they were undoubtedly communicating with themselves and future generations (maybe about animal behaviors, maybe about hunting techniques), there's a desire to attach significance to the "where" of where they were found—in a cave, in the dark. You are forgiven if you make the logical leap and consider these drawings as possibly the earliest recordings of human ritual anywhere in the world—indeed, the paintings are nearly fourteen thousand years older than Stonehenge and the pyramids and perhaps 7500 years older than Göbekli Tepe, one of the world's most ancient and well-preserved ritual spots.[12]

Looking at Lascaux's paintings, we witness some of the first steps towards non-oral cultural transmission. It seems evident (though it may not be so) that the paintings were used either as an initiation upon a shamanic path or for a passing of certain rites of becoming an adult. We'll never really know, but what we gain from knowledge of the existence of such a place is a touchstone to our shared cultural past. Even if not every human who currently exists is not descended from the humans who occupied that area, it represents the shared wealth of our species and is an important link to where we've been that helps us discover who we are now.

A nyancat will never do that.

Flash forward to today, give or take a few decades. In 1991, artist Felix Gonzalez-Torres famously bought billboard space across the country and posted a photo of an empty bed with the clear indentations of two bodies.[13] Gonzalez-Torres had recently lost his partner, Ross Laycock, to AIDS-related complications. There was so much cultural information transferred in that

---

12. Andrew Curry, "Seeking the Roots of Ritual," *Science* 319, no. 5861 (2008): 278–280.

13. Felix Gonzales-Torres, *Untitled*, 1991, billboard, figures 1–45. The Felix Gonzalez-Torres Foundation (New York), https://www.felixgonzalez-torresfoundation.org/works/untitled57.

one image, it was inescapable at the time. The United States was in the depths of ignorance and hate about the disease and its victims. The photograph was laden with implications that would have been obvious to most anyone at the time about the plight of the gay community and how forbidden it still was to be an out gay person. It captured the feeling of loss in a time when many weren't allowed to be in the same room when their partner passed away because they weren't family or allowed legal marriage. It carried with it the sense of loss of a generation of young people—brilliant, bold, funny, caring, loving people. Gonzalez-Torres himself died in 1996, also from a secondary infection caused by the disease. When we talk about art and its importance, *this* is what we're talking about. A drawing of a monkey with personalized colors and accessories is a trading card your friend makes you when they're bored, not a storehouse of economic portability. I'll take the long game on those odds.

As we've hopefully discovered (if we didn't know already), art is vitally important, as important as the blood flowing through our veins; without either, we cannot survive. It's also playful and something everyone should do, regardless of perceived skill level. So let's get art-ing.

Our use of art will be reflective, healing, as well as projecting. We'll use our art to figure out where we've been, process new thoughts about where we'd like to be, and heal parts of us that require healing and integration. With absolutely no ploys at modesty, I'm a disaster of a visual artist. Like all kids, I made my stick figure art but I probably progressed about fifteen minutes past the age of five with my skill at drawing. As a father, I can say with confidence that my five-and-a-half-year-old has surpassed me. Drawing is a talent I long to possess but haven't taken the time or found the right instruction that works for me to take it to the next (or any) level. Regardless, I still doodle; I make my own sigils and sometimes make a total mess with paints or crayons and then try to figure out what I've done. I sometimes use Photoshop to create art, mostly because Illustrator is too complicated for me. My own art may not hang in a museum or adorn people's homes, but that isn't what matters.

When I say that you can make art that is meaningful to your practice, I mean that *anyone* can do better than what I produce, and it works for me. In my example, I limited myself to visual art. I have also produced discordant music and fumbling poetry (and just wait until you see my dance moves). I'm a creature of many talents. It really cannot be overstated that it's important to practice different artforms because it's part of what it means to be human. The more we get away from the things that generate joy and cultural transference, the more we believe the lies that we're told, that only what monetarily enriches ourselves or others are worthy of doing. To fall into that trap is to lose the soul.

I'm not one of those witches who abhor money, just to be clear. Money is energy and its exchange has meaning, especially today. It is imperative that we support all sorts of people who are attempting to live fully with our money. Kind words are nice, but the money we give to artisans, artists, and craftspeople means the difference between them being able to create anything or not. In fact, I'd encourage you to support more people in the community than outside it—if this path is important to you, it should make sense that we need people who can create at a professional level in our community as much as we need to be creators ourselves. This isn't a ringing endorsement of capitalism, either, just a reminder to support those who struggle to provide what we'd like to see in the world.

What we're cultivating with this work in this book is the understanding that your joy can and should come independent of pressure to monetize it. Creation and the catharsis and joy that self-expression brings about should be their own motivations. Let's get started on bringing more enjoyment and healing into our lives!

Your Inner Child

When you were younger, what did you love to do? This isn't a "what did you want to be" question, as that often gets the anxiety ball rolling or at least gets people reflecting on their life and values and whether what they're currently doing match up (they rarely do).

"What did you *love* to do" is passion and action oriented. Maybe you loved drawing, collecting shells, or the early-childhood perennial DINOSAURS! (all caps, all the time for that one.) Maybe it was making houses or, as in my son's case, making "soup" from the mud, leaves, flowers, and rocks found outside.

Exercise
Childlike Grace

Gather up a pad of paper and some pens, pencils, crayons, or markers, whatever you have handy. You can work in your journal if you have a desire to keep your work together, but if you think your journal isn't large enough to allow your hands to freely move across the page, it might be a good idea to find something bigger. You don't want any inhibitions to your expression.

Take some time to revisit that passion from your childhood in your mind, but don't fall into nostalgia about it. We want to capture the energy of the passion as it existed, not as some gilded memory that doesn't reflect reality. Feel how engrossed you were in it, remember what it felt like to learn and stretch your brain around new concepts or engage in the pleasure of simple play. Really dig deeply into this; close your eyes if you need to. When you feel like you're fully immersed in that sensation, open your eyes and begin translating that sensation to paper. Just let colors flow while you stay in touch with the sensation. Change the colors as you feel inspired but keep it very free form, go with the flow. After you feel satisfied that you've completed your art, stop and assess what you've accomplished. Examine what colors you chose and reflect on what they might mean for you. Blues and greens can be tranquil or serene, yellows and oranges joyful, reds frustration and anger, but these are just basic meanings. Reds could also reflect the color of a favorite toy you played with or maybe it was your favorite color when you were young. Let your eyes wander over what you've done and assess. Did you fill the whole page from edge to edge? Are there definite, hard stops between colors or is it more of a gradient? Did your lines and strokes come through smoothly or jaggedly? How do you feel after this exercise? Content? Frustrated? Eager to do more?

Write down in your journal answers to these questions or other things that came up while doing this exercise.

Some may think this exercise is a little simplistic, odd, or childish—if you do, that's great, you've discovered the point of it. Our best healer is our own child selves, before our resentments, wounds, and scars built up and before we became jaded or disaffected. Children also live profoundly in the moment, there's nothing that compares to the intensity of a child focused on what they're doing right now. In most circumstances, that child-like state is quick to forgive, heal, and move on. They live in the state that adults train rigorously to attain spiritually!

To evolve ourselves and heal our traumas, we need to listen with the care of a child, see with eyes that shine with wonder and curiosity and give love wholly and unconditionally. Sometimes the best advice when you're feeling silly is to lean into it. Feeling silly is a warning sign from your adult mind that your behavior is risking scrutiny from other adults that may judge you for what you're doing, that you're risking "outsider" behavior that will get you ostracized. Guess what? Not a single person who has judged me for those reasons has ever had a meaningful or lasting impact on my life. Play is some of the hardest work you can do, and it's in that state of letting go that you begin making the greatest realizations and have the greatest growth opportunities available. Children are hard workers at play and you can be, too. With that said, let's continue our play.

From Art to Spellwork

Let's take the artwork we've just produced to our altar and do a little magick. In the playful spirit we've invoked, we'll end up using the results from our original coloring exercise as the backdrop for some sigil work. We'll explore two different methods of generating sigils, one more like guided meditation and the other more literal and straightforward.

Exercise
Meditative Sigil Manifesting

First, grab some scrap pieces of paper and a dark marker or other writing utensil that will show up against the other colors you've used on your paper. You can do this exercise at your altar space or wherever you feel comfortable; the intent is to get into a meditative mindset. Next, decide on a phrase that will empower your work. some suggestions include:

"I am a wondrous being of radiant darkness and light."

"I am free from the expectations of others."

"All eyes of judgment are turned away from me."

"I embrace my fundamental innocence and see the world with wonder."

Better still, make your own statements, using "I am" or "I have" rather than "I need" or "I want."

Settle your mind and perform the Heart Flame exercise. When you're deeply relaxed, recall that active state of childlike attention and excitement that powered your free-form coloring exercise. As you sit while breathing softly and evenly feeling relaxed and with your consciousness slightly adrift, focus on your mantra and see if you begin to get flashes of images. They could be shapes, lines, or fully fleshed-out pictures in your mind's eye. Staying relaxed, focus your intention around your mantra and let it guide you. If any images or shapes come up, simply draw on your scrap paper and continue meditating. Even if you see complex figures, places, people, or whatever else, draw a rudimentary representation, allowing your consciousness to stay in the flow—don't get distracted by the drawing.

If you've been waiting for a while and still don't think you've got it or if you need a little help, try calling to your mind's eye, tree roots. Gaze at the roots, see how they wind and curve and bend. Watch as they overlap one another and curve back again. See them curling and coiling, stretching out, arcing and leaping over one another. Recall your mantra, let it surround you and see the tree roots looping around and through your consciousness. In flashes and brief moments, you notice a shape pop out, a line, an angle, something that resembles a letter. Keep watching, and without removing yourself from this state, begin to draw what you see. Don't even look at the paper; you'll be able to clean it up later. If what you write down ends up overlapping with other things you've written, that's fine and may indicate a shape or sign that you should include.

When you feel like you've gotten all that you can from this exercise, set your writing utensil down and slowly bring yourself back to a normal state of consciousness. Stretch your arms, legs, and back. Gently roll your head and adjust yourself however you may need. Have a snack or a few sips of water. When you're ready, take your scraps of paper and begin assessing what you have.

If this exercise worked for you, begin assembling the various lines and shapes you received into a form you like and that feels resonant with the message you were focused on. Don't overthink it, let the symbols guide you to where they should go.

Exercise
Manually Creating a Sigil

In the event that the previous exercise didn't work for you and you're still staring at a blank piece of paper, we can get a little more literal with things. Nearly every sigil book or sigil introduction on the planet teaches one of the following exercises; they are very common.

Option 1

Take the mantra you wanted to incorporate, for example:

I am free from the expectations of others.

Go through the entire phrase and cross out the repeating letters and all vowels. Doing so leaves you with:

MFRTHXPCNS

Next, combine the letters into a shape that pleases you and reminds you of your intention. It could look something like this:

Figure 1

After you lay it out, you can start adding more to give it character or a personal touch, like this:

Figure 2

Option 2

Here is another way to create a sigil from what you have, this time using a grid or circle:

Figure 3

In this option, you trace letter by letter across the grid beginning with M to the F, to R and so on, until you end at S, giving you a unique shape. Tip: using tracing paper over the top of the grid helps you more easily visualize what you've created and isolates it.

Figure 4

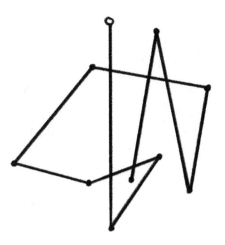

Figure 5

Whether you received images or had to create your own, now we're going to work on what you've received. Remember, the purpose of this sigil you've created is to give yourself an energetic zap that resonates your intention and is empowered through the joy and innocence invoked from the coloring exercise. Sigils may seem challenging at first, but ultimately what you're doing is empowering a shape to encapsulate an empowered feeling, message, or action. That shape is then given certain conditions for triggering or automatically releasing the intended result.

Exercise
Spell to Empower the Sigil

The final step is the actual empowerment. Using a lot of focus and energy, you build it toward a crescendo and then release it all at once into the object. Some witches and magickal people achieve this crescendo and release using orgasm, focusing all the energy as it's released into the sigil. Other methods are similarly useful, if that's not how you want to do things. In the next spell, we'll execute the empowerment in a more, ahem, subdued way.

For this working you'll need your altar space if you've set one up. If not, grab a candle, incense you find pleasing, the coloring, your sigil, and a dark marker or pencil that will show up on your coloring. If you've already drawn your sigil on the coloring, that's fine; if not, we'll do it in ritual.

Take a few deep breaths and relax your mind. Light your candle and incense, if desired, and then when you're ready, do the alignment exercise and the earth and stellar darkness meditation. Feel the radiant, ever-burning candle in your heart space being fed from above and below, making it glow hotter and hotter, shifting from red to orange, yellow to white and finally, blue. The energy of the cosmos and the earth unite within you and pool into a power you can use for your magickal work.

Set your coloring before you (with or without your symbol already drawn on it). If you haven't drawn it on your coloring yet, do so now, carefully recreating the symbol that represents the intention of freedom that you have earlier set.

Keeping your mind as clear as possible, channel the energy from your heart space and feel its heat slowly move across your chest, around your shoulder, tracing down the length of your arm. Really feel the warmth as it spreads around and down, and then sense it moving through your writing utensil and empowering the sigil as it is drawn. See the sigil glow with the energy you've summoned from the universe to empower your working. When you've completed your drawing, empower the artwork for our purpose. Say something like:

> *I summon the power of the universe and my own being to be present,*
> *the sacred three: you who are connected to the all that is, you who stalk*
> *the night among the spirits of flora and fur, you who move through the*
> *worlds of humans, unite in this sacred oath—I call upon you to empower*
> *this sacred sigil and let it be born into this world to do its work.*

Take three breaths of power and let each exhale breathe life into the sigil and awaken it.

Say:

Oh sacred seal, known only to me, I give you life and set you in motion.
Enhance my work and aid me in your special mission.

Now chant over whatever you created at the beginning (what follows is the example mantra from earlier) and use the full force of your will—make it count!

I am free from the expectations of others.
I am free from the expectations of others.
I am free from the expectations of others!

As you complete the repetition, send all the energy that you've generated into the sigil artwork. Give thanks to the universe and to yourself, sending a feeling of love or gratitude from your heart space. Take a few breaths to align yourself again. Give yourself time to feel sorted out in your body and blow out your candle and extinguish your incense. If you're having trouble reintegrating into yourself after the experience, try eating some simple foods or drinking a little bit of water or wine.

If you like, you can frame your artwork and keep it on your altar as a reminder of the working and the energy you put into it. Alternatively, you can put it away somewhere to keep it away from the eyes of others—it's up to you and your comfort level. Some even like to burn their workings to send it into the ether with a final energetic push. Personally, I think there's nothing wrong with setting it on your altar for a time and keeping it as a set piece to help anchor your work.

5.

Rewilding Your Soul(s)

Let me walk you through a typical morning routine:

It's just after seven o'clock in March and the sun has escaped the horizon but is still working through the treeline. It's a deliciously cool 63 degrees with low humidity, some of the best weather we get in south Florida. Every morning, I walk my wife and child to the car as they prepare to start their days. There is a palpable sense of promise for me in the morning. I look to the sky after my family leave and see wisps of feather-like cirrus clouds above. The beautiful blue sky will give way to storms in the afternoon. On my way back to the house, I stop by the side garden where I've slowly been building up a garden filled with native flowering plants and perennials to attract pollinators. Just last week there were countless monarch caterpillars munching the milkweed, all gone now, either picked off by lizards and birds or successful in hiding beneath a leaf somewhere to pupate. I say a little prayer that enough of them made it out of the larval state so another generation will be able to visit again but really, I know it's in the Goddess's hands, which is to say, nature. Orchid bees or green hoverflies sit stationary in midair, observing me. Over the years, I've developed a close affinity for these charming little visitors. Green hoverflies are a mimic species of orchid bees, so I've never been able to tell which they are. They are mildly social with me, and I always stop to hold out my hand in case they'd like a little perch. I'll say a few words to them, comment on some flowers that I think they should check out, and then, as you do with anyone you've developed a relationship, bid them to have a nice day.

This is probably the most magickal start to my day imaginable. The meditation, ritual, spellwork, and more will come later as needed, but this simple act of orienting and anchoring myself as a fully-fledged member of this place where I live, communing with plants, animals, insects, the air and sky, the earth beneath my feet—is magick.

Magick is inevitable, just as nature is inevitable. Since magick is part of nature, there's nothing that can prevent it from happening, and you must realize that you are a spectacular magickal being just like everyone around you. What you do with that knowledge will determine how much of a presence it maintains in your life.

As everyone is part of nature, we are all capable of using magick, and just like genetics cause us to inherit different traits that give each person a unique overall make-up, our magickal make-up is unique to us as well. Try as I might (and boy do I try), my mother will always have a better knack for plants than I do. They just thrive for her in a way that I can approach but not match. I've certainly inherited a heaping portion of affinity for plants and plant magick, but some people have a gift. And she'd never even consider calling what she does magick. Her cooperation with the natural world enables her to sense and feel what is needed without sentimentality (which is probably my biggest flaw when it comes to the plant kingdom).

Creating these in-roads to the animate world around us isn't so much forging new territory—this is territory that humans have tread from the beginning of our species, and likely much longer. It is re-membering. In the same way that Isis helped put Osiris back together (certain missing appendages notwithstanding), we are simply working to unwind the age of disenchantment of the last few hundred years. One of the biggest gripes I have with modern religious expressions is the "not of this world"-beliefs that are so prevalent. We are all perfectly flawed and in every way part of this world. No part of our biology indicates any other origin. This is your home, and you are likely going to have one of your souls energetically reemerge right here, hopefully not as microplastics that poison the ocean.

In an article on rewilding our local landscapes, advocate and author Emily Murphy urges us to:

"remember that we're not separate from nature but profoundly part of it. We are nature. When we take time to be in nature, watch her ways, and understand the interconnection of all things, we discover that when we think like an ecosystem, we can begin approaching nature and landscapes with more heart and know-how."[14]

What the "not of this world" worldview allows for is what we've got going on right now: overuse of natural resources without a thought for regeneration and balance. If we desire a different world, one that values nature, we must recognize our oneness with nature. We must feel the values of the ecosystem as part of our own bodies and value our bodies not as the machines that drive around our little egos but as things imbued with inherent worth and power.

Your brain is simply a part of the overall system; at times, it is a conductor of a symphony but not the composer. There's plenty of science to indicate that the gastrointestinal tract (called the enteric nervous system) populated with billions of bacteria have just as much an influence on emotions and decision making as our brain. It's even been referred to as our second brain.[15] What's even stranger to ponder is that those bacteria are part of our biology without being created by our body. They play an essential role in our health, behavior and functioning as an organism and our bodies simply couldn't live without them.

But wait, there's more! The intrinsic cardiac nervous system is yet another area that has been called a "third brain." This system contains a semi-autonomous network of nerves that coordinate and function strikingly similar to how neurons work in the cranial brain.

---

14. Kier Holmes, "Ask the Expert: Regenerative Organic Gardener Emily Murphy on How to Rewild Your Landscape," *Gardenista*, March 28, 2022. Accessed August, 2022. https://www.gardenista.com/posts/ask-expert-regenerative-organic-gardener-emily-murphy-rewild-landscape/.

15. Adam Hadhazy, "Think Twice: How the Gut's 'Second Brain' Influences Mood and Well-Being," *Scientific American*, February 12, 2010. https://www.scientificamerican.com/article/gut-second-brain/.

Whether created by our bodies or merely assistants in helping our bodies function, all these different systems give the "not of this world" viewpoint a cold stare.

So how do you move on from a materialist mindset? How do you embrace the wild nature of a native of this planet or universe? When estranged from what they truly are, how does a human re-member? Fortunately, the answer starts with you. You can decide right now that you want to rewild your soul, and we'll do it by going through the process of dying.

Dying So You May Be Reborn

Death is a squeamish topic for a lot of people; it can be uncomfortable to confront the reality of your own mortality. Some have already had a brush with death, a moment where the ego completely dissolved and left behind a feeling of great connection and unification with the all that is. For most people, however, the veil is firmly in place. We remain cocooned in our ignorance, encouraged by society to view death as something distasteful, unclean, or unnatural. Like many other facets of our life, we've been sold this idea by entire industries that sprang up originally to fill a need but then began to maximize occulting the practice so that our bodies become weird or disgusting to us. This change in view is especially true of the professions dealing with life's transitional states, those involved in birthing, being birthed, dying, or bearing witness to death. The same is true for every other aspect of medicine—a professional class exists due to public need, but our economy's nature forces it to exist behind veils of obfuscation. While this isn't always the case, it is the default model of operation. Reclaiming these areas of our lives is important, even if the only way we can do so is by researching and asking questions when we are in that environment. The health and death care systems in the United States are particularly opaque; I have sympathy for anyone trying to navigate them, including the practitioners who are stuck in the middle.

All that is preamble for what we're going to do next: experience a small, metaphorical death (no, not *le petit mort*) so that we may experience rebirth.

Allowing yourself to symbolically die opens your awareness to new possibilities and a greater appreciation for the universality of life and consciousness. The cliche that we are all one includes not only people or even living things but all matter. The matter used to create your body, your lover's body, your car, the spirit beings you talk to—everything around you came from a star that exploded such a crazy long time ago that it might as well be an infinity ago. Your ego might not enjoy the fact that all matter is infinitely recycled, but every other part of you knows that proton soup is our past and future. In the three souls model of understanding (i.e., talker, fetch, and holy daemon), there are elements of oneself that remain after the body dies and are frequently incarnated into other things, which is why ancestor work is such an important part of our practice.

Rather than experiencing a complete physical or psychic death, we'll be gently moving our awareness toward a more egoless place. Though our exercise will be different, it's similar in some ways to how Buddhist practitioners work to achieve a state of no-mind over the course of a lifetime in the pursuit of enlightenment. So when I say this is introductory, it's very introductory. For my own part, this is an important piece of my practice that I've been working on for many years and is based around acceptance rather than rejection of the material concerns of being alive and its consequences.

Exercise
A Small Death

This exercise is a brief, guided meditation. Get into some loose fitting and comfy clothes and remove anything that feels tight and restrictive or distracting, including jewelry—we want as few things as possible to draw us back into our bodies as we begin the light trance work we're about to undertake.

Begin by finding a comfortable spot sitting or laying down, whatever's most comfortable for you. Take slow, even breaths, allowing your mind to wander but not too far. When you've taken adequate time and feel that you're in a more relaxed state, draw in another deep breath and visualize the calm surface of a pond at night. All around is dense foliage; focus your attention on the pond. You feel safe, serene, protected. There's nothing else but you and the pond, reflecting the stars above. Everything is silent. Gaze deeply upon the water and allow your eyes to lose focus. Slowly, a star emerges just a hint brighter than the surrounding stars. You intuitively understand that it is Polaris, the North Star. As you gaze upon it, you see a wisp, a thread of light trailing up from it off the pond's surface. When you look up into the sky, you realize that it was the reflection of the same light descending from the star. The starlight stretches from the sky and the water, and eventually they merge, creating a milky, etheric path connecting the water below with the heavens above. You feel compelled to inspect this path and are surprised to discover the water's surface is hard, as if it's frozen. If you choose, you can easily walk across. Otherwise, you may stay at this quiet place and meditate on the star and the path.

If you move on, you see that despite ascending straight up into the sky, you can step onto this etheric, starlit way. When you do, you notice that the stars all around begin to slowly wheel about but the light path stays fixed. It's mildly disorienting, but the feeling passes and you feel okay to proceed.

You don't walk so much as drift along the path out into the cosmos. Surrounded by stars, adrift in the universe, you sense a loving presence. You know that this presence will watch over you and keep you safe as you make the journey away from your egoic consciousness. Slowly you feel your awareness spread out, as if your consciousness were water spilling out in every direction. You know that you are safe, but you also become less concerned about who "you" are. Very slowly, a feeling of intense connection ripples through; the nearby stars, sun, and planets of the solar system are all intimately familiar, and you experience a growing joy that fills you. It's almost overwhelming and just as it crests you are left awash with a sense of belonging and love. Love and connection. You are home.

Filled with radiance you bask in this moment until you feel the loving presence call you back to the starlit path. Your consciousness slowly retracts, but you carry a seed of this experience and know that just like a flower closes its petals after a day in adoration of the sun, you will be able to open yourself again and recall this feeling at will moving forward. In fact, this feeling has always been with you, you're only just now awakened to it. Protect this seed of deeper awareness and plant it safely in the soil of your consciousness.

As you return to the pond's edge, the light from Polaris retreats and the pathway evaporates into a fine mist that settles on the surface before disappearing entirely. Take a moment to reconnect with your breath—feel it anchoring you back in the physical form of your body and your awareness settling into yourself again. Gently open your eyes and stretch your body. Perform the grounding exercise from chapter 2 if you need. Have some food and drink, and move your body around to make sure you're well settled back in the present moment.

Now is a great time to journal about your experience, taking note of any key pieces of information you may have received during that time. Think about the following:

What did you learn from this experience? Were there any new insights you received? Were the sensations you experienced new? Did you feel a greater connection with the universe? In what ways, if any, was the experience akin to a death, where a piece of my former self was shed? Were there any frightening or unpleasant parts?

Pay particular attention to areas of discomfort, because they may offer insight into places that are ripe for growth.

If you come away from this work feeling deeply moved, congratulations! This is the first step toward deprogramming your psyche and awakening your souls to the depth of experience available for all humans. Guided meditations, journey, and trance work are a big part of this path that can be enriching and freeing. I recommend adding this working to your regular practice.

If you're more familiar with this kind of work, then you know how deep it can go. Adding in meditative practice, especially embodied meditative practice can help supplement the work. In the next section we'll explore some of these embodied methods for ecstasy that will help re-awaken the wild within.

Out of Our Minds and Into Our Skin

Now that we've had a taste of what it means to leave behind our minds, we'll look at some techniques for awakening our flesh. Like witchcraft itself, rewilding can be dangerous work—there's a reason that the chapter on healing precedes this one. Reawakening all the parts of yourself is the work of a lifetime but taking the first steps can be the most challenging. After all, most people in Western countries have spent a lifetime learning how to interact with and perform for institutions. The institutionalization of education has led to an enormous cultural shift, leaving children out of touch with their ancestry, their living relatives, and the natural world. When you begin the work of rewilding, it can create unexpected results. Most common is a well of anger that can be surprising and volatile. You're basically jabbing a stick into a psychic wound so deep that if you were to react *without* anger, sorrow, or fear it would be more surprising. If you feel like the emotions are becoming too intense at any time, take a break and work through the healing exercises again.

Witches new to this experience will want to make self-care a primary goal. When powerful emotions arise, write about them, take naps, drink tea, comfort your body and give it lots of love. Take part in pleasurable activities that make you feel good. It might be yoga or other forms of exercise, intimacy with yourself or a partner(s), or lots of talking with people who are sympathetic and understand the path you're on. This is hard work, take care of yourself!

Our initial exercise in this chapter was putting your consciousness in touch with the greater divinity of yourself as a being who is intimately part of the universe. It showed that when the ego dissolves or even softens, our materialist minds expect an end, but the shocking discovery was just the opposite! The discovery that "there is no end, nor beginning, there is only change" to quote a well-loved chant of the Assembly of the Sacred Wheel opens us to the mystery of all life and unlife. That mantra is something I've carried with me in good times and bad—during hurricanes, heartfelt reunions, health issues, the birth of my son, and through the pandemic. Rewilding is about opening to all your souls and acknowledging and nurturing them. Similar to how we learned to work with our demons rather than hide from them, the rewilding process is about discovery of your three souls and learning what they need. For your holy daemon, we found connection with the all that is, touching the limitless for a moment, unlocking the awareness of the timeless.

As you're striving to reconnect with your fetch self, your wild self, you'll likely begin to react with anger at how estranged you are from yourself. Just remember as you do this work: I'm no athlete and you don't have to be either. If you become healthier and more in shape as a result, that's awesome, but what we're focused on here is opening our awareness. How does it feel to take a long walk, and what forces have worked against you to prevent you from doing something so simple? When you do, what parts of your body hurt? Why do you think that is? Is it from your job, your daily routine? Time spent transporting your children back and forth to school and extracurricular activities?

Without judgment, assess how much you move your body. I'm not really concerned with physical exercise like going to the gym or doggedly sticking to a jogging routine; I'm more curious to know how much you personally get out of using your body. When was the last time you felt good in your body? These aren't trick questions designed to send you on a shame spiral. Step one on this journey is to start loving who you are, right at this moment, even if it's just to send a kind little hug.

Our next exercise will begin with opening up to what I like to think of as the feral soul, the fetch, or the shaper in the Temple of Witchcraft. The fetch soul is that which delights in the more experiential parts of existence, experiencing nature, eating food, having sex, making art and music, the thrill of hunting, of immersing ourselves in anything that satisfies us on an instinctual level. It's also a place where people find the greatest imbalances.

An unhealthy feral soul can be a source of unwanted or unhealthy behaviors such as addictions, violence, and power-over relationships and fear-based behavior that leads to all the above. A feral soul in a healthy state is a powerful thing and will empower your magick and your life. Left to its own devices, it can become monstrous. In fact, the argument could be made that the demons we began working with earlier arose from imbalance with this soul. I mention all this not to scare you but to give perspective. What our fetch desperately needs is connection with its natural environment. While I'm not a primitivist, connection with nature is something that has been lost in the process of industrialization and urbanization. To nurture the feral soul is to give it what it needs which is experiential contact.

Exercise
The Feral Soul

This exercise is a little different than others you've encountered so far. We'll engage in an activity you select and use it to seat ourselves fully into the feral soul. Some of the easiest suggestions are gardening, going for a nature walk, swimming in the ocean or lake, or even walking in cities if your circumstances or location make it impossible to do the above. Cities contain nature, and so is feeling the breeze on your face or the sun on your skin. Ultimately, you'll come to realize that sitting with your own body is nature itself but let's not get too far ahead.

For this example I'll use gardening, a particular favorite of mine that I do almost daily. After you do this exercise, I encourage you to take this approach with any activity you feel so inclined toward.

Establishing a Connection

Begin with the earth and stellar darkness meditation and use it to get in touch with the great above and great below, anchoring your consciousness in the world. Feel the energies of the earth and starry heavens pulling from each direction and anchoring in the center, your body. Take some breaths of power and set an intention to connect with and feed your feral soul, maintaining balance throughout the process. Whether you're entering an established garden or beginning the process of starting a new one, move into the space and begin assessing everything with your senses.

Take in the green of the foliage, any plants that are fruiting, the dark earthy richness of the soil, the sunlight's play across the landscape. Take in any animals, plants, insects or other creatures you see. Feel yourself absorb the energies of what you're seeing. Feel yourself being filled and enriched by the greens, browns, yellows and blues (of the sky) all around. Breathe in the colors and pull them down into the well of your being, down into the root, where the feral soul lives.

Move onto the sense of hearing. Sit quietly with your eyes closed for a time and once again absorb what you're hearing. Feast upon the delicious sound of the wind moving through trees, the purring of a sleeping cat, the distant sound of children at play. If your environment presents challenges such as traffic noise, attempt to sift through it for the sound of bird calls—yes, even pigeons. Continue through the rest of your senses as you feel called. Walk around to enhance your experience, and then stop and close your eyes to focus. Touch everything that wants to be touched. What does it feel like to run your hands over a mound of thyme? Through tall grass or over tomato leaves? Do you find yourself soothed?

Now that you've awakened your sensuous being and have fed all this delicious sensory input to your feral self, open your psychic senses and let them stretch out from your body. If you don't have much experience with using them, that's fine, everyone starts somewhere. To open your visual psychic awareness, simply allow your actual eyesight to lose focus and project your awareness over a plant. Likely, you will not "see" anything in the dense material world but will experience flashes of images that you may begin to stitch together into a message. Some people have better experiences with visual, auditory, or even tactile psychic awareness. You can listen for messages, feel for the subtle resistance of auras, or even be led by your nose to make new discoveries. Keep attempting until you find what works for you.

Plants are often eager communicators, so turn toward a specific plant and try to get a message from it. You may get information about the state of its health or it may have a request—and no, it's not always *water me!* though that will happen—sometimes it's *can you get this other plant's leaves out of my patch of sunlight?* Or *can you move that rock closer (or further) away from me?* Listen to what the plant has to say and if it's asking for reasonable things, fulfill its requests if you're so inclined. As mentioned, messages may come to you in different ways so keep your senses and awareness open. Relationships are built on exchange, which builds trust, just like with animals or other humans. Don't worry about getting it wrong, just keep attempting.

When you feel ready, thank any plant spirits that you've made contact with and bring yourself back to normal, waking consciousness.

It is important to always reflect on the experience you've had and write down any key information you received. If you experienced any challenges, write about those. As you work more with the nature spirits around you, you may notice patterns that help draw attention to different alterations you should make in your approach. My experiences usually include a mix of images and emotions, small compulsions, and sometimes scent. Over a very long time, I've learned to interpret my collected experiences.

I'll work and attend to plant spirits by communicating back in a series of images and emotions. I'll also vocally speak to them as I'm doing this. I greet them in the morning while I'm watering and ask them how they are. I'll comment on things I see and ask them for feedback. At the time I'm writing this, I have some tomato plants that are just about at the end of their lives. They've provided at least thirty pounds of tomatoes for me this year, so I've been giving them a little more love and attention as their time winds down. I'll miss them when they're gone but I'll plant their seeds in autumn and welcome a new generation.

For a while you'll doubt yourself, thinking *is it all in my head?* but as you continue your relationships, you'll start to see something come of them. You'll come away feeling energized, like your body has been nourished just by spending time with them and listening to them. Your plants will start to look healthier, they'll respond to your presence, your voice and start communicating with you much more quickly. This practice is also a great first step toward working with land spirits. They are much more finicky and less trusting than domesticated garden vegetables, for sure.

Exercise
Conscious Movement in the Environment

As we build our practice, we'll experience deeper ecstatic states that put us even more into connection with our wild soul. For now, continue this practice as regularly as possible to help cultivate the connection to what your feral soul needs. What follows here are other practices you can work on. Try them out, see what reactions you get, and keep a journal of what happens.

Walking

Do not underestimate the power of a long walk. People tend to go for walks as a form of exercise, which is fine, but a soul-enriching walk is different. The key here is walk slowly, take your time, and stop often. If something catches your attention, go check it out. Through an absorptive sort of observation, you will begin noticing and communicating with all sorts of things. Animals will appear seemingly out of nowhere and the subtle play of life will become even more apparent. Allow any of the strain, stress, or preoccupation melt away with each step. Visualize that tight, anxious energy going down into the earth; in return, receive refreshed, renewed energy. Don't worry that you're putting "bad" energy into the ground—the earth will filter and renew that energy. Think of it kind of like psychic composting: what's unneeded or unwanted is taken, broken down, and turned into fresh and fertile energy.

Swimming

Depending on where you live, the summer months are a great time to do this practice of absorptive observation while immersed in a body of water. Because water, especially ocean water, casts off negative ions, it can quickly elevate your mood. Take time to immerse yourself in the water. In much the same way that we "ground out" our negative energy on the walk in the previous exercise, water can do similar things. If you can, completely submerge yourself underwater and open your psychic senses for an amazing experience. There is so much life in water, and the spirits of water are sometimes easier and faster to reach out to than land spirits. They're also a lot more confusing because their objectives and motivations seem a little more alien to us land animals. Attempt to focus on just one thing in the environment and open your awareness to it. See what images come to mind, and allow yourself to be open to any messages you might receive.

⊢ ◆ ⊣

As you can see, any activity done thoughtfully and with careful attention to the environment can become an enriching experience that opens your connection to your feral soul.

6.

First Contact:
The Spirit of Your Land

"First contact" is a phrase loaded with connotation. In our post-1950s space race era, it implies first contact with an off-world alien species that has flown in their faster-than-light saucer to start abducting people in remote parts of the world. We're going to apply the term in a slightly different way here, however.

When you think about where you live, what springs to mind first? Is it a cultural identity associated with your background? An association with the city or community you live in? The mountains, rivers, forests, plains, or deserts that make up the natural world around you? While culture and community are wonderful things, the latter is what we're focused on in this chapter. Even if it's a city, the place you live in, the natural world around you, has certain characteristics that define its personality, in a sense. Things like elevation, how water cycles through the environment, types of trees and vegetation, animal populations, weather patterns, and seasonal changes that affect all of the above collectively come together in what's called an ecoregion.

Ecoregions can be enormous, extending well beyond the borders of entire states in the US, or they can be quite small, spanning no more the circumference of a small collection of islands such as the Florida Keys. We'll delve more deeply into ecoregions in a later chapter but for now, this is the scale I'm talking about when I mean meeting the spirit of the land. These spirits are often ancient, and even though you are a part of your local ecoregion and thus part of the whole that is the spirit of the land, they can often feel quite foreign and occulted from your normal state of being. They have personalities, needs, desires, and manners in which they like to be appeased. Very few know how to interact with them, so it will be practice of discovery for you filled with experimentation and documentation.

Journey to Meet the Pulsing Heart of the Land

Meeting the land is a powerful and moving experience. In some ways, you can't prepare yourself for what you'll encounter because it's just so huge. Sometimes it seems that people's experiences with gods and goddesses have made it possible to tune out or turn the volume down on what they're interacting with. There's a general tendency to personalize or "make small" the gods even though they are quite vast. Most who work regularly with a particular deity already know the enormity of what they encounter because they've done it for years and years. It's the blind man's elephant metaphor, where feeling along in the dark, you stumble upon a trunk and think you've found a snake, or find a leg and think it's a tree trunk! Years of work and devotion uncover something else entirely in so many unexpected ways. But it's the bite-sized approachability of the gods (and their general or at least initial anthropomorphism) that serves as an in-road to greater and more meaningful relationships and experiences. When you meet a land spirit, it's not always that way. Meeting the spirit of a place, meaning the Spirit of Place, can rattle or even fracture your perceptions and assumptions of reality. For me, this is a fundamental experience of being not only a witch but a well-developed human, but others will disagree and that's fine for them. Some make clocks while others live outside of time, but I digress. Many years ago, I had just such an experience.

A friend had a residency at the Everglades National Park and invited my wife and I to come stay for a weekend. I had experienced parts of the park in the past but was at a particular spot in my craft where I was just beginning to actively cultivate relationships with land spirits. The park is absolutely stunning, especially in the winter months when the mosquitos aren't as thick. We walked a trail through dense foliage one evening, only able to see the path from the edges of our vision. It was one of those experiences at night where when you look directly at it, it disappears. Just the smallest fraction of moonlight came through the canopy and all around the sound of gators, making their bullfrog-like grunts. Suddenly about halfway through the trail, fireflies lit up, flashing all around. All I could do was gasp—this was the first time in probably a decade that I had even seen fireflies, which are not too common in south Florida. Here I was on this impossibly dark trail with the very real threat of alligators all around, and I felt like I was floating among the stars in the universe. I had lost all sense of self for a few moments and just bobbed, stupidly, to the rhythm of these insects. For those brief moments, there was no me anymore. Just the vast sea of existence without limits.

I hear those of you familiar with will-o-wisps, by the way.

And that wasn't even *the* encounter with the land spirit, but it had primed me. My subconscious was coming untethered. We awoke before sunrise the following morning with a planned trip to a cypress dome where an 8- to 10-foot alligator had been spotted the day before. The sun rose on our way to our destination, a deep red ball emerging from the edge of the grassy edge of the world. We stopped at a lookout point, and I thudded my heavy boots across the wooden planks, my mind still on the previous night's experience. I was a bit lost between the present moment and tangled thoughts about everything. "There's so much life here," I thought, feeling uneasy for some reason. Creeping on the edges of my consciousness was an unfiltered recognition of just how massive the concept of life was, how infinite and all-encompassing it could be. As I looked across the expanse of the river of grass, past distant cypress, I felt and for one of the few times in my life, saw the spirit that was the embodiment of all of that life. For a few moments, something impossibly enormous labored across the horizon; it was like watching a mountain move. It was a darkness, something that felt enormously old and a little Lovecraftian. I felt it reach out to me across the distance, and then it exploded into a murmuration of birds. Staggering and leaning on a railing to keep my balance, I was left gasping for breath. I could still feel this presence and knew that it felt me. A recognition and a giving had occurred. It was awe-inspiring and deeply moving while at the same time ripping me from my moorings. The very soul of the Everglades had appeared to me, and all I could do was tear up and try not to vomit. From that point forward, I knew that as long as I lived in this place my magick would be linked to it.

We continued to our destination, walking through a half mile of not-completely-dried-out swampland before arriving in the cypress dome. That was its own magickal experience, but I was preoccupied with what had happened earlier.

The living spirit of the Everglades had touched me, and I felt as if I had been electrified. Very frequently my encounters with spirits of this sort have made me feel quite ill for a time, no matter how much grounding or centering I've done before or after. I should probably have shielded myself when the experience happened but it was so quick.

Afterward, the word "feral" started popping up in my writing; for weeks and months, I felt as though the energy of the Everglades had unleashed something wild in me, something that at first felt misanthropic but I later determined to be a rebalancing. The scales had been squarely tipped in humanity's favor for quite some time, and now nature, the Goddess, was looking for emissaries to work in Hir highest interest.

The only way I can really describe it is a very short, very powerful burst of radiation. Having no meaningful protection against that much energy can be hard on the body. Take a lesson from me: if your spidey-senses are tingling, it's best to put up a shield and maintain it. In hindsight, my nighttime walk among the dancing lights and threats of death should have been a clear indicator for the sort of experience I was about to have. For my troubles, after we left the cypress dome and drove back to the house where we were staying, I was barely able to get the door open before some severe vomiting episodes.

It's not easy, but these are the sacrifices you make sometimes when you pursue an ecstatic and embodied craft. It's not always dancing and singing and self-possession.

In all, I've had experiences like this probably a half dozen times, maybe less. Exposure to raw power shouldn't be done without care, and unexpected things do happen, so pay close attention if you are in these situations. After you have such an experience, reflect on how it made you feel. Was there anything out of the ordinary that preceded your personal event? You could certainly backtrack minutes before, but go further—what about hours or even days before? Go back however far you can to the point where you think, "You know, that was really the point after which the out of the started happening."

A noteworthy thing that comes from my own experience: time is mutable, and these energies begin to unfold before the main event, so to speak. The energy almost seems to seek you out across the barriers of time and space. It disrupts the normal feel and flow around you. In a more recent event, I became quite ill and dissociated from my body before an event occurred, a first for me. The event was planned, so I suspected immediately what was happening and used the tools at my disposal to allow the unpleasantness to pass so I could be present to fully experience the event. Those feelings are the sort of tip-offs ecstatic witches look for because if they are ignored, they can make a person very reactive and lose control of their energy, magick, and mind. There's a difference in degrees between losing control to open ourselves to the work and losing control of our power entirely. Becoming unhinged makes you a liability to yourself and others.

Familiarizing Yourself with Your Land Spirit

Let's take a walk through your local ecoregion. Head outside and take a walk around anywhere: a city street, a walking trail, a pocket park, or a national park. Get outdoors and leave the comfort and insulation of your home. Don't worry, I promise we'll come back; I'm a Taurus, after all, so we'll have plenty of time to burrow under some blankets and drink tea while eating bread and cheese.

As you walk around, feel the energies of the earth flowing up through the soles of your feet as you release whatever is negative or unhelpful to be grounded by the earth. It's difficult to do, I know; I'm always taking pictures when I'm in nature, but for this exercise leave your phone behind or at least in your pocket. I feel that the spirits of the land often move slowly or at a different wavelength that requires uninterrupted attention and focus. As we began doing in the last chapter while interacting with plants in our garden, now turn on your psychic senses, whatever allows you to know things, even if you're not sure how they work right. It could be intuition, the power of observation, or something else. To paraphrase author Raven Grimassi, who himself was likely paraphrasing Matthew and Luke from the Christian Bible, ironically, listen with ears that can hear, look with eyes that can see. If you're familiar with the sensation of adjusting your eyes to be able to see Magic Eye puzzles, imagine doing that but with your senses. Some people get impressions that come through almost like memories; others might experience audible or visual sensations someone like not actually hearing something but thinking they did. Frequently, I'll see a being for just a moment before it reverts to a more mundane object: the being will appear and then shift into a tree stump, a clump of mushrooms, or fire hydrants, among others. I also regularly receive messages via images broadcasted to my mind's eye, things that are inexplicable based on my lived experience and clearly not originating from my own senses. When any of these things start to happen, I know that I'm both in the presence of and have gotten the attention of local spirits. Now the fun begins!

Exercise
Contact

The first part of this exercise is for you to decide: Think about where you feel most drawn to in nature in your ecoregion, somewhere you can easily access and that you consider representative of where you live: a river, forest, desert, mountain, ocean or lake, you get the idea. I recommend a place that feels as though it has a presence (like my Everglades adventure), but make sure it's near enough that you can come back at least a couple of times a year to continue working together and deepening your relationship.

Before setting out, plan on bringing some common-sense things you'd take with you on a mundane journey outdoors: sunscreen, bug repellant, plenty of water, and so on. And because this is a journey with a magickal goal, you'll also want to bring some things that have personal meaning for you, such as a pendant that reminds you of your commitment to the craft, a rock or small pouch of dirt from your home to help ground and remind you of who you are and where you're from. You'll also want to bring an offering that seems appropriate, and importantly, unlikely to pollute—a small amount of ground herbs (no seeds!) or spring water are the best options. Some people like to bring fruit or other food, but depending on where you are, the seeds from the fruit could unintentionally take root, and food is generally eaten by local critters who are much better off eating the food native to their environment. I also like to bring a small palm stone that aids in opening up my psychic awareness (labradorite and lapis are two favorites that travel with me regularly).

The idea is to focus your awareness, open to the energy of the environment around you, and contact the subtle energies that will help guide you. Sometimes, as in my Everglades experience, the spirits come looking for you, but that's not always how things go down.

When you arrive at your place, prepare yourself for unexpected things. Settle in and ground yourself, do the earth and stellar darkness meditation and prepare your energetic shields (mentioned in the Key exercises chapter).

If you have a particular spot in mind that you strongly feel captures the spirit of the place or that seems to have an energetic resonance, journey there. If not, walk around. If you're in a national park or another large, wild area, take some trails or do what everyone else who comes to enjoy the area does. Keep your senses open. Eventually, you will home in on where you need to be; you'll turn a corner on a trail and be faced with an odd-looking tree or suddenly, almost as if by accident, start noticing strange details in the landscape around you. These are great indicators of spirits at work trying to get your attention. When find the spot, make yourself comfortable, sit (if you can), and begin meditating. Remember to keep your shields up but open your awareness to receive any messages or information you may need. If you start feeling like it's not working, you can stand up again and keep moving, but really give it a fair shake before you do.

Land spirits can come in many forms and have many roles (something I'll delve into later). Right now, attempt to make contact with the over-soul or overarching entity that encompasses this place similar to trees, where each tree has its own spirit but there is an oversoul for birches or aspens. Another way to consider it is your body is made up of billions of cells. Each one has a unique role and duty within the body *and* each also helps comprise you. At the same time, each cell has genetic information that makes you uniquely identifiable. In this exercise we're looking for that entity. If you're in the Midwest, for example, it's the entity comprising all of the streams, hills, maples, black walnuts, oaks, rabbits, snakes, and so on.

When you sense that you've made contact or suspect that such an entity is near, leave out the offerings you've brought. Say aloud or communicate through your psychic senses that this offering is for that being. A lot of times what you'll encounter is something primal, something that feels almost elemental. Don't be surprised or discouraged if you can't have a conversation with it, and don't be surprised if it's not keen on whatever offerings you leave.

The point is to attempt contact, maintain respectful behavior, and give a wide berth for the sake of safety. Think of this exercise as you would attempting to befriend a large brown bear or a gorilla (not that you should ever attempt either). You would start by getting the animal comfortable with your presence before attempting closer, more intimate contact.

You will know when you've made contact, believe me. One of the unique things that happens when I make contact that I've heard other witches mention is something I've started referring to as "fractalizing." When an overwhelmingly powerful entity draws near, I'll often see it first as a collection of fractals of different colors. They'll slowly form patterns that eventually resolve into the being, almost as if my mind cannot comprehend what it's taking in and must break it down into its most basic parts to make sense of it. This may or may not happen for you but keep it in mind if you're having trouble assessing what you're interacting with. As I've said, my senses tend to be more aligned to vision, so that's my most frequent way of receiving information.

After your experience, think about how it worked for you and journal about it. How did the entity reveal itself? Was it passive or active with you? Did you get any information or receive anything else from it? Be careful as you process that you don't put anything on it that wasn't actually there. The mind has a desire to fill in gaps so just be aware of that.

Now what? Keep fostering that relationship and begin to foster others. Now that you've had the experience, it will become easier—though the experiences themselves are no less challenging and fraught—to meet them again or to begin the practice with the land around your home. If you're like most humans, you live in a city, which means that spirit of your personal piece of land might be much smaller and easier to communicate with. As you continue your work, you may start to partner with the land and using it to empower your magick. This process is slow and must be done with the utmost respect. If it's not done for the mutual benefit of the land and yourself, reconsider what you're doing because you'll be acting from a place of extraction, not a great place to work from.

Anthropomorphism and You

One of the pitfalls a lot of witches fall victim to is anthropomorphizing behavior. This is where someone will say they spoke with a non-human entity and had a fully formed conversation, complete with tell-tale signs like human emotions. There's something to be said for interpreting a conversation you've had with a spirit so that it makes sense to other people. Being a good interpreter is a necessary part of hedge riding but it's a skill developed over time, done haltingly, and with caveats. Anthropomorphizing your experience is easy shorthand, but it also can create misleading dialogues. I'm always more inclined to believe someone who says, "I think the spirit is saying this, and there's a welcoming feeling coming through with the message" rather than, "I spoke with the spirit of the woods, and said it was mad about all the garbage people leave but I told it we're witches and it said it's happy we're here!"

In my experience, large entities of place are quite primal, but smaller, more short-lived beings are chattier and more apt to have a better understanding of how to communicate with humans thanks to more regular contact with us. There are also the entities who live beside us who most never see, such as the fey of historically Celtic regions and various beings such as trolls, dwarves, and giants from areas historically occupied by Germanic tribes. Almost every culture has these kinds of creatures because they're very real, living in their hidden civilizations with their own rules and customs. Is it anthropomorphizing when we're interacting with them? It's hard to say, because humans have interacted with these beings so regularly (including documented encounters) that it seems like a case of spiritual co-evolution.

My personal interactions with these beings have been varied, from non-communicative shadow spirits that seem eager to be magickal parasites to witches, to literal forest and swamp dwelling "people" who are playful tricksters but can communicate fairly well and be very helpful when they want to be. My son will frequently look for gnomes when we go out for walks and enjoys the fun energy they seem to embody for him.

We may wonder if anthropomorphizing is good or bad, but I think the question leads us to a more important question: is it accurate? In the realms of little (or big) human-like entities, it seems fine. Land, plant, and animal spirits usually operate outside of the human-like spheres and have their own cultures and methods of communicating. Err on the side of caution and always be honest with yourself and others, and you'll come out better and more respectable in the end.

7.

The Decompositional
Magickal Model

One of the closest allies for those on the path of the moonlit hedge are fungi. Humans have lived and died, been nourished and inspired by and even been consumed and recycled by our seemingly most humble relatives on this planet. What we don't know or understand about mushrooms and fungi in general could fill volumes. I equate our understanding of the fungi kingdom to the discovery of dark matter, in that we know there's something pretty fundamental we're missing but we don't know what we don't know, a paradoxical turn of phrase from the Iraq war coined by Donald Rumsfeld. War criminals might be a good example here as they represent a certain kind of rot that threatens to take down all of the infrastructure around them. This is where the mighty mushroom comes in. As accumulators and transformers of things that sicken our world, they disperse pollutants and modify them, breaking down deadly compounds and releasing them into the metaphorical forest floor for uptake and consumption by trees and plants.

Applied to your current circumstances and given the right energetic push, you can see how this might be a useful technique for a lot of thoroughly bad people or situations. Because there's nothing quite so inevitable as the breakdown of organic matter and that will serve as the impetus for the breakdown of magickal energy as well. Put in concrete terms, if someone tries to hex you, imagine how useful it would be to collect all that energy, drink it up, and spread it around like fertilizer. Mind the mushrooms.

Animist thinking gives us both real interactions with spirits and inspiration from how these real-world denizens behave in their environment. A fun place to start with mycological work is a standard guidebook. Through regular observation and active investigation (complemented with book learning), you can find rich magickal inspiration.

Mushrooms are the fruiting bodies of the overall organism of fungi, which have an entire underground web of mycelium which can sometimes stretch for miles and interact and communicate with plant and animal life across the expanse of their bodies.[16] The roots of trees and all sorts of plants have generally beneficial interactions with the mycelia (themselves very much like roots) where messages are passed from tree to tree in one species or across many species. When a tree in one part of the forest contracts a pest or disease, all of its local neighbors find out because of messages that are sent with the help of fungal mycelia. Even more astonishing, its neighbors are able to send reinforcements in the form of nutrients or other chemicals to the affected tree via the mycelium.[17] While the mycelial network of *Star Trek: Discovery* is fictional, the concept of a network that connects the whole forest together becomes much more believable. If you've ever wandered through the forest and had the sneaking suspicion that you were being watched, you can add the entire mushroom kingdom and all the trees in addition to the forest spirits as potential observers. The forest is less a dense accumulation of vegetation and more a collection of eyes upon eyes, ears upon ears.

Another *Star Trek: Discovery* thought before we move on: they introduce the viewer to the strange idea of an interdimensional network of mycelium that somehow spans across space and even time. While the fungal space network has yet to be discovered, it's a great model for an adventurous witch to take on. After all, what is psychic phenomenon other than bilocation of your own senses across time and space? How useful would it be to use the myce-

16. Taryn Plumb et al., "Mushroom Extracts: The Mycelium vs. Fruiting Body Dispute," *North Spore*, October 14, 2020. https://northspore.com/blogs/the-black-trumpet/mushroom-extracts-the-mycelium-vs-fruiting-body-dispute.

17. Peter Wohlleben, *The Hidden Life of Trees: What They Feel, How They Communicate* (London: William Collins, 2017), 121–122.

lial model to guide you there, rather than simply homing in on your target? We should probably stop here because we start getting into extremely theoretical models where questions come up such as, can you create these bilocational models between you and a friend? What about you and spirits or gods? What if instead of drumming up the energy to recreate the universe at the beginning of every ritual, there was immediate interplay between you and whatever spirit with whom you've created this relationship? On its surface, it sounds like an excellent way to become a kind of avatar, but there are a lot of dangers to consider, chiefly among them: do you open yourself up to the potential for permanent possession it could imply? It might constitute a form of chaos magick that even chaos magicians recoil from!

Mushrooms and Magick

Let's set aside deep thoughts about relinquishing control of your earthly body for now and get back to some more grounded (literally) topics—mushrooms. To quote *Discworld Almanak* by Terry Pratchett: "We can assure our readers, whom we wish to preserve, that there are only two facts to bear in mind when selecting fungi: ALL FUNGI ARE EDIBLE. SOME FUNGI ARE NOT EDIBLE MORE THAN ONCE."[18] As you taking your own mushroom almanac around with you, keep this in mind. If you find yourself tempted to consume them as you journey through this decompositional model of magick, remember that even the most skilled mushroom hunters make mistakes sometimes. Mistakes in the mushroom world can make you very sick or very dead. If of the mycological madness has you hankering to chow down, go to the store and get some.

Mushrooms have a long history and association with nature spirits, the underworld, and journey work. The indigenous people of Siberia as well as the Saami people of northern Scandinavia and Russia were said to do healing journeys and trancework utilizing the fly agaric mushroom. The indigenous Mazatec people of current-day Mexico ritually used psilocybin-containing mushrooms, a practice that is believed to be the gateway that introduced

---

18. Terry Pratchett and Bernard Pearson, *Discworld Almanak: The Year of the Prawn* (New York: Doubleday, 2004), 39.

them (intentionally or not) to the modern world.[19] In Europe is a long history of association of mushrooms with the fae, gnomes, dwarves, and all manner of earth-associated creatures.[20] The history is intriguing and hints at how little we know of the history of the normal people who worked with these beings.

Partnering with Fungi

The best way to start work with mushrooms and the beings who appear when you work with them is sitting with them, meditating with them, and opening your psychic senses to the messages they may have for you. This method is the same for just about any spiritual entity, too. Relationships of exchange create relationships of trust. When you start to identify some of the more common mushrooms in your local biome, you can greet them, and send energy to them. And when you observe what they consume, you can start to bring offerings of food to them.

There's a stinkhorn that sprouted up in my faerie garden that I particularly love. The fruiting body only lasts a day or so, but I know the mycelia are there below the surface. Stinkhorns are pretty common now, thanks to spreading through mulch bought at home and garden centers. When I first noticed it, it was (no surprise, given its name) by scent. They can smell pretty foul; some have described the scent as rotting flesh, but to me it's more like bad clams and bleach.[21] For weeks I searched and searched for a sign of the mushroom until one day I saw the unmistakable form of *Phallus impudicus* (its Latin name, if that gives you a hint). It was just on the cusp of casting out its odd, balloon-like structure that sends spores into the wind. Funnily enough, they've been called Witch's Eggs too, with some sources even describing them as semi-edible in their just-emergent phase, when they are said to resemble

19. David Nichols, "Psilocybin: from ancient magic to modern medicine," *The Journal of Antibiotics* 73, no. 10, 2020.

20. Mike Jay, "Fungi, Folklore, and Fairyland," October 7, 2020. https://publicdomainreview.org/essay/fungi-folklore-and-fairyland.

21. Eleanor Phillips, Jennifer L. Gillett-Kaufman, and Matthew E. Smith, "Stinkhorn Mushrooms (Agaricomycetes: Phallales: Phallaceae)," UF IFAS Extension, December 17, 2018. https://edis.ifas.ufl.edu/publication/PP345.

eggs. In China, stinkhorns are cultivated for consumption and are said to resemble the taste of hazelnuts. However, stinkhorns are extremely difficult to tell apart from the emergent phase of the aptly named death cap mushroom, so, semi-edible or not, I'll be saving my appetite for safer comestibles.

What can we learn from these things, and how can it be applied to our magick? I keep a compost bin, even when I'm not actively using it. To have that hot, steaming, living nature close at hand is vitally important. Compost provides nutrients from our waste matter to plant life. In a time where soil nutrients are being wiped out by destructive farming practices, compost fills a gap usually reserved for industrial fertilizer.

Mushrooms act in a similar sense to compost in soil—they don't mind! Fungi will quickly move in and rebalance when everything else has gone sideways. My cute little stinkhorn loves to spread through deep mulch or leaves, sending its fibrous roots far to help break down vegetation and make it into nutrient rich soil. A long time ago, I'd get distressed whenever a mushroom would pop up in my garden, thinking it was a sign of some moral failing on my part. Now I know that it's one of the best signs of vitality you can come across.

If you haven't heard of or read Paul Stamets, he's an amateur mycologist who arguably knows more than anyone on the planet about the role and potential of these outstanding organisms. If you want to start thinking like a mushroom and using the mycological model to power up your craft, he's the best guide you can have.

Exercise
Making Friends with the Mycological World

Hopefully now you have some thoughts on how to partner with fungi and some ideas around the magickal applications they might have. Next, we will delve into a little mushroom magick of our own. Getting your hands dirty is the absolute best way to learn anything and if you haven't figured it out yet, I'm all about dirty hands.

What follows is a multi-step process of discovering, communicating, harvesting, and utilizing a mushroom friend from your own environment. You'll end up with an amulet for protection that uses the filtering, transmuting power of fungi, rather than deflecting negative energy away. Instead of acting as a shield, it will absorb that energy. By absorbing it, the fungi will then use it as the fuel which then empowers your protection.

There are a couple of resource-dependent tasks needed to set this exercise up. It's not as easy as some magickal creations we'll work on, but the challenge of the hunt is part of the fun. The first task is to find a living mushroom specimen. There's a very obvious hack that involves going to the grocery store—if you decide to do that, it's fine. However, I would say that if you go the grocery route, buy the dried mushrooms for reasons mentioned later that will expedite the process.

If you're the old school type of witch who may be carrying a toad in your dress pockets, then you're probably the type who likes to work for your magick a little harder in the first place, and you'll always be your faery witch-father's favorite.

Find a Specimen

To begin, go out in nature. Don't forget to bring a small container and a reusable water bottle both for your thirst and as an offering. Poke around in grassy medians, parks, or wooded areas little or big. There's an above average chance that as you're walking around sticking your nose in the business of plants and trees that you'll come across some sort of fungi. South Florida is a place of particular abundance in this regard due to the amount of regular rainfall and the areas of ground saturation, rotting logs, and the like. If you're curious where to find wetlands near you, the Center for International Forestry Research has an excellent, searchable wetlands map detailing where to find them all over the world.[22] But you don't really need a detailed map because mushrooms and fungi have adapted to just about every climate, including deserts.

Take an afternoon and walk around, and while you're out looking for the diminutive sex organs of our soon-to-be allies, use it to take note of other things around you, such as the kinds of trees, plants, and animal life make

---

22. Center for Forestry Research Wetlands map. https://www2.cifor.org/global-wetlands/.

up your biome. Indeed, certain combinations of all three will be clues in the future for what sort of mushrooms you may find nearby. This is no master-class on mycology, and I am definitely no expert, so chances are good that you'll find something and have no idea what it is. Generally, in suburban areas, you're likely to find the ubiquitous little brown mushrooms, puffballs, shelf mushrooms (which look like shelves on tree trunks,) slime molds, or some variety of what is largely called a toadstool. The toadstools are an unscientific classification but usually what people think of when they think of finding mushrooms in the wild. They have the classic mushroom or umbrella shape and may or may not form in fairy rings—what look like gatherings of mushrooms that form a ring or perimeter, many times with empty space in the middle where no fruiting bodies are growing. As I've intimated earlier in this chapter, identifying mushrooms is challenging even for the most sea-soned mushroom hunter, so always err on the side of washing your hands and don't carry anything you gather in your mouth.

When you've spotted a mushroom it may be tempting to yell out, "I've found a mushroom!" You may want everyone within a mile radius to know you've found something and give you all the space you need. But instead of grabbing fistfulls of mushroom and running away cackling, it's more polite to sit and quietly observe your mushroom.

Silliness aside, you want to get a sense of why these fungi chose this loca-tion to expend the energy to fruit here and send out spores with the hope of reproducing. Observe carefully to see what sort of medium it's growing out of—grass that gets heavy fertilizer? Woodchips from mulch? A rotting log? There's a genus of mushroom called cordyceps that infect different kinds of insects and parasitize their bodies. They're hard to find, but it's amazing to see a mushroom growing out of a dead ant's head.

Take notice of any other plant growing nearby that might contribute to your mushroom's overall lifecycle. Is there animal waste or evidence of birds such as ducks, geese, or herons? Remember that fungi spend most of their lives as mycelia beneath the earth in long fibers that grow and intermingle with roots of plants…not unlike the etheric cords from an earlier chapter. How might the fruiting body you're observing be aiding the plant life around it?

Mutual Offerings

Once you have found your specimen, it is time to make a connection. Hold your hands out and try to feel the energy moving around and through this organism. Does it feel fast and hasty or slow and deliberate? Where does it feel like the energy is coming from, and where is it going? Become acquainted with the mushroom as best you can. Take pictures to assist you in identifying but don't worry about it if you aren't sure—it's hard to do! Finally, feed some of your own energy to the aboveground mushroom and the mycelia that make up its true body beneath the earth if it's growing from the earth.

If it sounds scary to offer your life force to something you've never met, consider that you already do this daily in countless ways. Every time you work for someone else, you are giving them an offering of your personal energy in exchange for money. Every time you help a friend or neighbor with a chore or task, you're offering them your energy as a gift to maintain right relations. The offering of a small amount of energy to someone with whom you're trying to build a relationship is normal and healthy, just as we discussed in the last chapter.

If you're still not convinced and want to experiment more before doing so, please do, this is your path to walk and learn as you see fit. But do leave an offering, in this case some of the water that you brought along.

As you did with the spirit of the land, try to get into a comfortable position and open yourself up to all of the entities of place that are living, dying, and reproducing all around you. Since you're a little at the mercy of where you were able to locate your mushroom friend, you may be in a something of an exposed area where people might see you doing something they don't normally do. That's okay because generally, I've found that people tend to act like they've happened on someone doing something intimate and avert their eyes and change directions. While I am sympathetic to your discomfort, I encourage you to remember that the path of witchcraft is one of challenge by ordeal, and one of the earliest challenges we face is being comfortable doing witchcraft.

On the scale of lighting candles to summoning goetia (demonic spirits), I think it's easy to see where sitting with a mushroom and maybe saying some things to it lands. The more you own it, the less important it feels to other people. But act like you're doing something strange or gods forbid, wrong, and people will eagerly agree with you.

Anyway, sit down with the mushroom and introduce yourself. Talk about why you're there and maybe offer it some flattering words while you do. "My, what a slender stalk you have," or "oh, your gills are so beautifully spaced!" "Your cap looks like a perfect place to take a nap, if only I were small enough!" You get the idea, but don't be insincere…if you've never taken the time to truly appreciate the miracle of a mushroom, now's a great time.

I used to loathe spiders, something I learned from my mother's arachnophobia. I was never scared of them as she is; I just found them creepy and gross. Then I took the time to observe them in their webs, watch their precision and their baffling ability to plan and weave such perfectly symmetrical patterns. I had never seen them for who they were and never bothered to understand them as beings in this universe who are just as important and deserving of a spot in the sunlight as me. I had a moment of feeling love as I watched the banana spiders living their lives, a feeling that you'll know when you step outside your prejudices about the world and engage it with the wonder of a child.

As you look at the curves, scales, vulva, skirt, and gills of your new mushroom friend, open yourself to awe. Feel gratitude for what you're experiencing and love for this miraculous being in front of you. In some ways, adjusting yourself in this way and having these feelings is the energetic offering because it means you've extended beyond the bounds of your anthropocentrism. It's okay if you're not there yet, but we'll be exploring these ideas and feelings in the next chapter as we expand our work with spirit guides.

Feeling the Energy

Take some breaths and center yourself. Feel the warmth of the ever-burning flame in your heart space and focus on it. Pull energy from deep within the earth and out into the starry depths of the cosmos. Bring them together and use them to add energy to the flame. Feel its warmth extending outward, vibrating through your being, feeling like the thrum of your heart, resounding through your flesh and outwards.

Take a moment to sit with this feeling, knowing that it is a manifestation of your true power as a witch, and that it's available for you to use in whatever ways you feel are appropriate.

Extend your hand just over the mushroom so that you are close to it but not touching it. With your body vibrating at this elevated space, see if you can feel the mushroom's aura. Can you can feel its signature or energetic resonance touching against your own etheric body? As with many energy interactions, the feeling may resemble two magnets of matching polarities bouncing off or repelling one another. Try scanning around the mushroom with your hand and see if you can get a sense for its own etheric body or aura. Does it follow the shape of a single mushroom or a grouping of them if they're clustered together? Do you pick up anything from the parts of the mycelial body you can't see that may be threading through what it feeds off, like a rotting log or beneath the earth?

Now try sensing other things from the mushroom. Do you get any imagery or flashes of feeling, sound, or color when you scan it? Take note of any information you get because in time it will help you start to develop what is essentially a personality profile of the living being you're working with. If the mushroom doesn't like something you do, if you get a feeling that it is pushing away or feeling agitated, take note of what that was that you were doing. It's important to understand that just like with people and animals you encounter in life, the spirits in the world are just as apt to feel good, bad, or indifferent about you.

Having overall positive relationships even with those who feel indifferent or worse toward you can make all the difference in how easily you make your way through the world. Even if you get back that this particular being doesn't care for you, remain polite, thank it for its time, and even offer it some energy if you're given permission.

Once you've scanned the mushroom and taken notes on what you noticed, ask it if it would like an energy offering from you. For now, use your words;

as you progress with this work, you'll likely be able to psychically communicate with the being in simple ways. Don't expect an audible response from the mushroom, but definitely take note if you do. As mentioned in the last chapter on anthropomorphism, it's best to receive the message the being is sending in the purest form possible. As much as possible, try not to overlay your own personality and use of language on something that clearly doesn't communicate as we would.

When you ask to give the mushroom your energy, try to send the image of what you mean from your mind—visualize energy flowing from your connection and going to the fungi for its own use. If you get what feels like agreement or consent to your offering, reach down into the well of your heart space and allow the energy to flow along the channel of your arm. Very similar to when you used the energy to sense the aura of the mushroom, you're now going to extend that energy and let it flow into its aura where it will mingle and be absorbed.

Broadcast a sense of gratitude as you offer your energy, something akin to the loving feeling you cultivated while observing it. Let that gratitude flow with your energetic offering. In all, you should only offer just the smallest amount because what you're doing is giving thanks and helping to build a relationship; no more energy is required than that for now.

Get a sense for how the energy was received. Pour out a little bit of water at the base of the mushroom as an offering. Think about the water's purity as it seeps down into the body of the fungi and helps to ease the electrical pathways it uses to send communications.

Exercise
Your Mushroom Amulet

To make an amulet, you will pluck one of the mushrooms that you've been working with but first, we're going to ask for permission. For the most part, any fungus or plant whose reproductive organs you offer to take and spread around via spores or pollen will be overjoyed at the extra help. That said, it's never polite to take without asking.

This work can be completed in the same sitting as the previous exercise or can be done in a follow up visit. The best way to ask is similar to how you've communicated with it already: imagine seeing your hand, knife, or whatever you're using cutting or breaking off the mushroom and carrying it away. Send it a message of spores spreading on the wind as you take it away.

Wait for a response. If you sense that you're getting a definite feeling of assent, proceed with taking the mushroom. Take a moment to thank the fungi for its sacrifice and give a little verbal blessing before you leave, such as "Thank you, mushroom kin, for your sacrifice. I honor your power and presence. Hail and farewell." Don't forget to actually tap the mushroom cap after you leave with it, staying true to your promise.

Create a Protection Amulet

When you get the mushroom home, set it somewhere to dry out for a few days in a safe place that gets exposed to the air. As it dries, it will likely lose most of its mass and become very shriveled; mushrooms are mostly water.

While you're waiting that part out, you can use the extra time to source a good home for your new friend. Consider how you might use it in the future. Is it something that you'd like to keep on your altar, working as a sort of battery for any protection or warding and whose reclaimed energy will be used as a source in your spellwork? Or do you want it available at any time, wherever you are? If so, something you can wear such as a locket might be better. Lately I've seen some practitioners have started encasing herbs, stones, and whatever else they want to use in acrylic resin. It looks kind of pretty and it will definitely protect your specimens from rotting due to exposure, but I tend to shy away from encasing anything in plastic because it doesn't feel right to me. Remember that this magickal tool will be performing a dual task: capturing any negative energy that comes our way and transforming and storing it so we may later use it in our spellwork or other magick.

As you think on ideas for your amulet, you may want to consider adding stones of power or plant allies to the mix as well. Consider stones such as black tourmaline will create powerful boundaries, and selenite will cleanse energies as they arrive on your metaphorical doorstep. Thorns cut from roses, blackthorns, hawthorns, or (if you live in the southern US) bougain-villea can also help to create harsh impassable boundaries. Note that some thorny plants are not native to where they are found; keep this in mind if it is important to you that any plant you use in your magick is endemic to where you live. Personally, I like to use what is close at hand and easy to access and many non-natives fit that bill.

In the example that follows, I use a small cloth that I'll work into a sachet and fill it with some of the ingredients listed above. Later I may empower it with a little sigil magick as well. It is written to empower your wards (if you haven't done so, an exercise in the Appendix called Creating a Ward, page XX will show you how). I like to use black for warding work, but choose a color correspondence that works for you.

If you really want to supercharge your working, wait until the dark moon is drawing near and use it for its natural boundary-setting abilities. You could also tap into the Saturnian energies of Saturday or the astrological hour of Saturn for a similar purpose. Try out different auspicious timings as they're available but if the need demands that you move forward without them, do so.

When you're ready to begin, gather everything together and go to your regular altar space. Light your candle and some incense, this time taking care to select an incense that can be used to cleanse (I like a mix of frankin-cense and myrrh). You can also use whatever you typically would to cleanse space; just know that this will be used for purifying the energy of our spell ingredients.

Empowering Your Amulet

Lay out the mushroom in the middle of your altar along with the square of fabric, some twine cut to about 18 inches in length, and any other items you intend to put into the sachet.

Take some deep breaths and let the energy of the incense bring you into the dreamy presence of ritual space. Start by centering yourself and per-forming the earth and stellar darkness meditation. Pull the earthly and stellar energies into your heart space and feel them expand. Let the energy flow down your hands as you pick up each item and run it through the smoke. As you pick up the cloth for the sachet, feel the energy run from your hands into the fabric, and feel the fabric awaken.

Say:

Awaken, sachet fabric.

Reserving the mushroom for last, pick up each piece you're going to work with and do the same.

Now, take the mushroom and gently wave it through the smoke.

Say:

Mushroom ally, I awaken you and ask for your energies to be present in my work of creating an amulet. I ask that you lend your power of taking negative energy and cleansing it so that it may be reused, and that you work with the wards set around my house. I invite you to be an honored guest in my house and help guide my path as a spiritual ally. So mote it be!

Feel your new mushroom spirit ally awaken and be enlivened and attuned to the task you have created for it. If you are using any other items, awaken them in a similar way, asking for their energies to be present and lend their power to your working.

Take all the items that you have awakened for this task and gather the sachet fabric around them. Use the twine to start winding it around the top of your sachet and work your way down the loose ends, leaving a little excess hanging out so you can tie it off when it's been fully wound. As you wind the twine recite this chant:

Twine, wind and bind,
Seal and unite,
Twine, wind and bind,
And charge this rite.

Keep repeating the chant as you slowly and tightly wrap the twine around, making sure nothing falls out and that any accidental openings are properly sealed off. You'll want enough string so that you can wrap it tightly just underneath the contents and completely cover the loose ends of the sachet. When you hold it up, it should vaguely resemble a mushroom with the twine-wrapped part resembling a stem.

When you've finished, tie off the string and lay it on your altar space. Say:

> By the power of the witch, sovereign of this land, I charge you
> with catching and recycling harmful or unwanted energy directed at this
> household and its occupants. I charge you to store the recycled energy so that it
> is available for this witch's work. I ask that the Spirit of this land, my
> spirit allies and ancestors (and any god/desses that you work with)
> bless this work if it is their will.
> Awaken to your purpose, mushroom ally, awaken to your purpose,
> Amulet of the Fungi Kingdom!

Now take three deep breaths and blow them into the amulet, while envisioning it coming alive to the task you've given it.

Congratulations! You've just created life! What a proud parent you must be! Seriously though, it's important to treat what you've made here as you would any other beings or entities you encounter—you've given it consciousness and used other beings to compose a unique entity that hasn't existed in this world before.

The animist thread of the particular practice of the Moonlit Hedge considers this being as no more or less important than any other you might encounter, including humans!

Care and Feeding of the Amulet

The needs that it has are minimal though but to keep it healthy and active towards its purpose, you may want to feed it every now and then, around the full or new moon are a good time, not for any real auspicious purposes but mostly just so you have a regular time you establish for yourself so you don't forget though you can do extra workings aligned with either, including the dark moon as mentioned earlier in this ritual to enhance its barrier-creating abilities.

What's involved in the care and feeding of a magickal construct? Usually spring water, smoke or if you want a special treat, you can use a few drops of Florida water, I've included a recipe at the end of this chapter if you'd like to make your own.

When you feed it, do the same thing you did when you created it: pull energy into yourself and then use it to awaken the amulet. You don't need to awaken it again but sending a little energy as you drop some spring water on it, and call it by its name (above we called it the Amulet of the Fungi Kingdom, but if you named it Hieronymus, that's cool, too). You can say something such as the following:

Imbibe and thrive,
Amulet of the Fungi Kingdom,
be refreshed and quenched,
may you remember your purpose.

Now you can use your new amulet—keep it on your altar or even hide it somewhere in your house. Often magick folks will create a comfortable home for poppets or other animated objects, such as a padded box or a glass display case if you're not worried about prying eyes. When doing spellwork, bring out your amulet with all the pomp it deserves in what feel like appropriate moments. Ask the amulet to release a portion of its stored energy for your stated purpose (gods help you if you've got a lot of enemies, that could be a lot of energy).

Moving On

If there ever comes a time when you no longer feel that you need this amulet, you can cut the twine and unwrap it. As you do so, say:

I release you from your task, Hieronymus. I release you from the work of this witch, I release your energy back into the universe to follow its next purpose.

Take all parts of the bag and dispose of it off of your property, preferably buried so that the earth may quickly absorb the energies. It's traditional to bury used, consumed, or released ritual items at a crossroads; if there is a crossroads near you that would work for this purpose, there's something satisfying in adhering to the traditions of magickal workers through the generations.

Finally, as we launch into the next chapter on spirit guides and allies, you'll want to maintain a connection with the fungi who sacrificed one of its fruiting bodies for your work. It's good manners to honor the goodwill that took part between you two, being very different species, especially since you're using that being's magickal energy on a long-term basis. Once in a while, revisit the area in which you harvested the mushroom and reconnect with it. Offer it some water, some of your energy if you like, and if it's grown more fruiting bodies, offer to take them and help spread their spores around. If you have questions that you think it could answer, ask. First try sending and receiving images from it. Don't be afraid to work with this new ally away from where it lives. You have, in essence, made a spiritual connection with this entity and made an agreement to work together. If the relationship deepens beyond that point, you may want to consider making a pact and taking them on as a personal guide, something covered in the next chapter.

Florida Water

Florida water has a long history as cologne used by people of all genders with the original trademarked recipe dating back to 1802. Over time, it became closely affiliated with hoodoo traditions and has proven to be such an effective way of blessing and cleansing space that it has found its way into many witchcraft and other spiritual practices as well. The name comes from an association with the legendary fountain of youth, rumored in the early Spanish colonial era to be located in Florida. This is a variation on my go-to recipe for Florida water. My recipe uses roses more heavily than the typical formula which has sweet orange as its base.

Recipe
Florida Water Recipe

- 1 quart of high proof grain alcohol
- 1 to 2 cups dried rose petals

- Essential oils:
  - 12 drops ylang ylang
  - 4 drops sweet orange
  - 4 drops bergamot
  - 4 drops cinnamon
  - 2 drops lemon
  - 2 drops clove bud
  - 2 drops lavender
- 1 quart spring water (preferred, if you can freely source it)

There aren't too many springs in my neck of the woods so I often just use filtered water as I don't want to support companies who steal spring water and sell it back to people.

Starting with the high proof grain alcohol, look for something with more than 75 percent pure ethanol (151 proof)—the higher the better. People who went to college for reasons other than gaining a degree will know very well which brand to look for. In a pinch I've made it with vodka, but since vodka is 100 proof, i.e., 50 percent alcohol, you don't need to add water at the end, which means you'll need to spend more to create the same amount of product. Up to you.

Make an extract with the alcohol and rose petals (when alcohol is used as the base, it's called a tincture). I used to gently simmer the rose petals in the water and then strain and pour an equal amount of alcohol, but I think the method of alcohol extraction is better for preserving the essence of the rose petals.

If you've never made an extraction, it's very simple: Get a large, clean jar quart-sized or larger (more is better if you're an exacting sort that wants to have exactly a quart of tinctured alcohol at the end). Put the rose petals in and top it off with the alcohol. I *highly* recommend buying certified organic rose petals, or better, getting them from your garden. In the past I've had to throw out batches of rose tincture because the rose petals were from a metaphysical store that sold products sprayed with a dye, which is not something you want to be spraying on your body or breathing in. I also wouldn't use anything from a flower shop, because the flower industry notoriously uses crazy amounts of pesticides.

Most canning jars have rudimentary measurements on the side and can be sealed fairly well to avoid alcohol evaporation. I do *not* recommend water bath canning or pressure canning unless you are keen to set your kitchen on fire—just tighten the lid by hand. Keep it somewhere darker and cooler, a pantry or kitchen cabinet are fine. Every day or so, give it a shake. There's a lot of different methods and philosophy around making tinctures but since we're not using this for medicinal purposes, we'll keep it simple. After at least a couple weeks take out your jar and open it up. Give it the sniff test—does it smell more pleasantly of roses than it does of hooch? If it's satisfactory, strain out all of the solid material using a fine mesh screen lined with cheese cloth. Tincture accomplished!

Now pour off your new rose tincture into a clean half-gallon sized jar and top off with your water. If you're making less, adjust the recipe but keep it easy on yourself. The final step is to add your essential oils and of course, witchcraft.

I like to leave the jar with my finished product out overnight under a full moon to soak up those lunar energies. I'll perform a blessing on the full jar as well.

The final step is to pour it off into bottles. I'm not sure how much truth there is to it, but some say that ethanol degrades plastic and leaches out chemicals into the liquid. It makes some sense as alcohol is a solvent, but it's generally a good idea to avoid plastic. Yes, it's ubiquitous but reducing the amount of it in our lives is an overall positive, especially in your witchcraft. So go for glass bottles.

You can store your Florida water in the big jar long term; because it's about half alcohol, it will last pretty much indefinitely, especially for our non-medicinal purposes.

8.

Meeting Your Spirit Guides, Allies, and Other Fretful Beings

Here's another experiential story from my adventures:

I'm walking through two feet of standing water on a memory of a trail. It's oven hot, and humid, but the water that I'm wading through cools me down. The only sound I can hear is the water sluicing by as my legs and walking stick break the stillness. Minnows and mollies dart ahead of me in the water, making quick breaks to the left or right to avoid me. This is snake and gator country and I'm in a hyper vigilant state, scanning the cocoplum bushes to either side of the trail and trying hard not to wander off where I think the trail might be. This is not the best frame of mind for doing, say ... deep trance work—this is the survival state, the heart beating steadily but quickly, the eyes dilated to catch the first sign of threat is its own ritual state.

As I walk along, I take frequent breaks. I change my speed in order to creep more quietly through the water. In a clearing surrounded by cypress trees, I catch sight of a few deer drinking water and munching on grasses that break the surface. They see me but are unperturbed, probably because of my distance and the fact that deer have become creepily more domesticated since I was a child. I watch them while leaning on my walking stick for a few minutes before pressing on. In this instance, I've made some pretty classic mistakes. I didn't tell anyone where I was going, I left my phone in the car, and I don't have any water. Even in a park that's as relatively small as the one I'm in, there is a lot of trail, and given the water conditions, it's pretty unlikely that I'll see another human the entire time I'm out here. I also have a bad ankle that has tripped me up in the past in this same park, which forced me to hobble two and a half miles back. Fortunately it was much drier and easier to navigate then. In other words, don't be like me, kids.

On my journey today, I'm going to see a special tree. Trees are amazing spirits to work with, though finding ones willing to work with you can be challenging. Sometimes you can find a tree that really is the anchor to a place or that has a certain clout with the other beings that inhabit a place. That's the case with this one: it radiates a centrality, it has an almost royal countenance and it's also old, maybe one of the oldest trees in this waterlogged park, and it's pretty obvious that it's dying. It's fairly close to the trail, and when I stumbled across it, I was in awe. It was eager to connect and share, an oddity as eagerness is not one of their common traits. The unique part about this tree is that it seems especially attuned to people who walk with one foot in the spirit world. There's nothing I've discovered about its past that would explain why—it just likes us. Visiting it is akin to visiting a friend. When I see it today, it's the same as every time, more pits in its bark tell the story of its rapidly declining health. Insects and fungus are going to work on the ruddy exterior that is responsible for glucose transfer from the leaves down to the roots (this is pretty simplified but how I understand it). Communication has been very halting from this tree but there's a joyful energy exchange that it does with witches and other spirit folk. We basically come into contact with one another and just exchange glowing, happy energy, like sitting on a park bench with a lifelong friend, sometimes the pleasure is just in sitting quietly with someone you feel connected with. Two beings, enjoying watching the world, together.

In spite of my bad ankle that can make it treacherous to visit, I try to make this trek at least a couple times a year, knowing that time is relatively limited. This dedication is part of what it means to have spirit allies and guides. The physical presence of this particular tree is so important to me and yet because of our positive connection, I can draw on its wisdom and energy to guide my work as a witch and healer from just about anywhere. In doing so, I connect with this particular tree but having the relationship that I do with it has empowered me to connect with its species. Connecting with the species on a spiritual level is connecting to the guiding oversoul that animates all trees of that type. Ages ago there was a graffitied painting on the side of a building in Chicago of André the Giant with the words "André the Giant has a posse" beneath it. In a similar way, my tree friend has a posse, and our relationship means I'm rolling deep with all its kin.

When you start developing these sorts of relationships, you'll often find a plant, animal, particular rock, hill, fae spirit, or human spirit whom you kind of vibe with. If you keep in contact with them, over time you'll start to notice that they share more with you, allowing you to begin experiencing the power of a species' oversoul. This connection doesn't always happen, however; sometimes there's just a funny water spirit at a particular creek you vibe with and it just stays that way. When I first noticed that tree and how it reached out to me, I thought it was just that: a one-off thing where I'd made a friend. But over time, it has changed to include a better understanding of its species, their unique presence in Florida, and what they bring. The species has become one of my spirit guides over time who make up a small collection of very close beings in a sort of network of trusted advisors. You can also develop a network like this, too.

South Florida has a wild and sadly, rapidly changing landscape. I've touched upon it before but it bears repeating: it is a truly magickal place on par with any of the other magickal centers of the world but humans are despoiling it. While I appreciate that lots of smaller urban areas are in a similar process of change, to give you a sense of how dramatic the shift here has been, nearly a thousand people a day move here, based on data gathered by the state of Florida.[23]

Chances are good that you also live in a place that is rapidly changing either from human occupation or involvement in another way. Climate change will force a lot of uncomfortable changes around the globe, and wealth and land concentration into fewer hands will contribute to it. For this reason, it's so imperative to at least meet the beings who have been your neighbors all along. Try to make those friendships while you can—it could very well be the difference between saving a species, its individuals, and its oversoul. One of the

---

23. Office of Economic and Demographic Research of the Florida Legislature, "Florida Population and Components of Change," Demographic Estimating Conference Florida Demographic Forecast, July 18, 2022. http://edr.state.fl.us/content/conferences/population/ComponentsofChange.pdf.

messages that myself and many others in the witchcraft and magickal communities have received from our gods, guardians, guides and allies is that this ear is of fundamental importance for our species and the direction that the earth takes as a whole. Some have received messages that we are on the cusp of a global transformation, that ascension on a spiritual level will become more and more commonplace until the point of critical mass is reached and it shifts the power dynamics of this world. I like that idea, though I have to admit it's hard for me to see what is happening through the fog of selfish ignorance that denotes this time so well. But I'm also a Taurus and I have a stubborn adherence to what I believe in. If others much wiser than myself are forecasting an outcome of comparatively enlightened beings as the cosmic ages turn, then I'll work toward that goal. And in the belief of that goal, each of us makes it more possible. So get out—meet your neighbors and let them know that it's a worthy cause to stop indiscriminately killing insects, plants, and the wide variety of beings you encounter because they are, in fact, beings.

Beingness in the Spirit World

What is meant when we say "beings?" I've already tossed the question around with an implication that you know what I mean. And really, if you are a critical reader, you've likely already inferred the meaning. Beingness is the natural state of matter in our universe, as consciousness is imbued within all matter. To have consciousness, in whatever form, is to be a being that can be interacted with.

If you tune out the programming that considers all things as objects—a viewpoint that forces everything to be broken down into quantifiable little bits—it makes perfect sense. But if you believe or see that there's an order that amounts to something other than pure chaos in the patterns of the universe, you start to take the first turn toward beingness. Consciousness makes a lot of sense when seen as a field that interpenetrates all matter; it's simply a natural state of matter in the universe in that it has always existed and that something within our brains is attuned to that field in a way that is unique to humans. Consciousness in rocks or rivers or sand crabs looks different because each has its own way of attuning to that field. The consciousness of

Jupiter or a cloud are different things but both tap into the same fundamental aspect of matter.

I won't rehash the entire argument, but it's from this characteristic of matter that beingness arises. If everything you encounter has its own consciousness, even if it presents itself in an incomprehensible way to your senses, it still is a being and something with which you are capable of making real connections. It's the most dismissed argument against pure materialism by people who land in the materialist camp, but fortunately it's not my job to convince them. My job is to open your eyes, my dear witch friend, to the concept that everything you work with is already functioning in this way whether you know it or not. I'm just the guy pointing the way to your own realization of this fact.

If you want better, more effective spell results, you'll know that it's not simply the energetic field quartz generates that lends its energy to your desired effect—it's that you are making a request and an agreement with the spirit of that particular piece of quartz that it will assist you. In the same way that you can still get milk from a cow you don't think or care about other than on a mundane level, you can still use that quartz for its inherent traits. But if you love that cow—if you pet it, genuinely have affection for it, and are invested in its happiness—you'll get better milk and a new friend. The same sentiment applies for a "simple" rock as well. Much like we started the work of creating a mushroom ally in the last chapter, continuing that work with every being you encounter is fundamental.

Before we begin exploring, I want to make one last point: if you're someone who has experience with magick, consider your work during ritual or when creating spells. You may have lists of correspondences, e.g., rose quartz for love, bay leaf for success or money, black salt for warding or banishing. Maybe you anoint a candle with some essential oils. (I know I do, a lot!) But how does it feel when you look up a correspondence and see something like rhododendron oil? If you're like I've been for most of my magickal life, I said, okay, slathered it on and never thought about it again. And if you're able to move energy and follow the flow of a spell, it probably worked for you. For me, there was always a sense of flatness to the whole thing though. I was looking for a feeling of (booming, echoing voice) *real witchcraft*. And it was kind of there or else I wouldn't have kept at it. But I found when I was familiar with the ingredients that I was using, and even better, when I had done meditative work to get to meet and know the beings I was working with, I noticed that the energy awakened. In other words, I saw the spellwork come alive in a way I hadn't noticed before. By including plants, stones, crystals, and other things with which I had a personal relationship, the energy of the spell had awakened. It was therefore easier to accomplish my working's goal because I had cooperated with beings on the spirit realm to aid me in my work. What's more witchy than that?

Working with Various Spirits

Communing and working with spirits is very enriching work, but who are they? Some are allies, some are just spirits, and others are frightening. There are numerous kinds of spirits that we'll be discussing in this chapter and all are tied to the land in one way or another.

There are flora and fauna, the spirits of the animals and plants that live in your area. There are land wights, a term I use to describe spirits of a particular place that are not necessarily related to flora and fauna but are still definitely tied to the land. Think of regionally or culturally specific spirits such as fae in Celtic mythology, dwarves and elves from Norse mythology, djinn and ifrit from Middle Eastern folklore. Spirits like these live everywhere and becoming familiar with them is essential. Finally, there are the dead, who can include your ancestors, or not. Sometimes you need the help of a powerful ally such as a judge, if you need to win a court case. If you've worked on fostering that relationship ahead of time with a judge buried in a local cemetery, you could ask them for their help.

The best advice I can give for meeting spirits is to research: Find preserves and parks that are undisturbed or that are being rewilded. Get books on native plants, trees, animals, fish, birds, and other wildlife in your area. Look up your local ecoregion—the EPA has an awesome guide with all fifty states mapped down to what are called Level III and Level IV ecoregions.[24] From there, you can find the descriptor for what your region is called. For example, I live on the edge of the Eastern Florida Flatwoods and the Miami Ridge/ Atlantic Coastal Strip. Using those names, I can start doing research to help me identify common species in each ecoregion. Look up hydrological maps to see how water might move through your area and to help find subterranean water flows.

Also look up the history of your area: identify where historically significant events happened, where the areas of culture are or (especially) were. Find where all the cemeteries are in your city or county and plot them on a map. Even if you were born and raised in a specific area, it's surprising how much new information you can discover when you start digging into research. The best place to find a lot of this info should come as no surprise: the library. The default now (including myself) is to start with Google searches and letting that be the extent of any research. I'm going to be the annoying old person and say that's not good enough simply because most of this information hasn't been digitized due to libraries being grossly unfunded. Libraries often have historical info that dwarfs whatever city or county government agencies have, and there's usually at least one librarian in the system for whom this is their special passion—they usually leap out of their skin at the opportunity to assist someone with their unique skill set.

Now that you've identified some resources and started reading through them, take some notes. If anything sticks out at you, write it down. Find a species of medicinal plant that grows natively in your area? Write that down. An endangered species of bird? Write it down. Someone famous or powerful buried in a forgotten cemetery? You know the drill.

As you work up your list of potential spirit "targets," write down some of the details you've learned: Do they live near rivers or lakes? Maybe they like ground that is high and dry. If one of your targets is deceased and you plan to visit their grave, is there anything you could bring with you that

---

24. United States Environmental Protection Agency website, "Level III and IV Ecoregions by State," last updated May 2, 2022. https://www.epa.gov/eco-research/level-iii-and -iv-ecoregions-state.

could sweeten your interaction with them? Maybe there's (literally) a sweet they were said to like, a poem they were fond of that you could read, or they were often seen wearing blue clothing so you could bring a scrap of blue fabric. Spirits of native plants tend to be a little less fastidious about the kinds of offerings you bring but as you work with them, pay attention—they may occasionally surprise you with an odd request. As our rapid population growth has exploded over the last two hundred years or so, the opportunities for people to interact with spirits have also increased; so you may run into a spirit who has a taste for cornmeal or brown liquor because someone else made that particular offering in the past. Keep your senses and your mind open to all possibilities.

We started a couple chapters back with a local land spirit because it's a biggie; although going from easy to challenging might be the better way, I think the opposite is true with this particular work. There's no guarantee that things will get easier; sometimes the most innocuous seeming spirit can lead you on quite the detour away from where you thought you were going. This chapter continues with work on meeting and making new friends, allies, spirit guides, and land wights, and how to work with the dead.

Some of the tools needed for this work include: an easy to carry bag or satchel, a water bottle for drinking, a smaller bottle in which you can bring water that has been consecrated to use in offerings or cleanse tools for workings (a travel-sized bottle is good), a small bottle of alcohol (drinking not rubbing) to use for offerings (again, travel-sized bottle size is adequate), an oil or spray used for consecrations (such as the Florida water in the last chapter), some empty bottles and jars and plastic baggies for gathering if the need arises, a knife, maps of any wilderness areas you're considering visiting (in case you get lost or spirit-lead to an area and need to return to the trail), snacks (you don't want to have a hangry, low blood sugar moment when meeting spirit allies), a notebook and pencil (look for a notebook that works in damp weather, they're everywhere online). Don't forget other practical things to bring along: bug spray, sunscreen, a good hat, a walking stick, a flashlight, a compass. And it's always good practice to let someone know where you're going and an estimate of when you'll be back or when you'll call them to let them know you've safely made it out of the wilderness. All the supplies and suggestions listed above are flexible based on where you're going—there's no need to go overboard if you're just hitting up the park across the street!

If you like, you can return to the same area where you met your land spirit, but it's not strictly necessary. Sometimes it's fun to explore new areas and see who shows up. Of course, the research you've done earlier will be helpful in setting up some targets. Your first few times out, you'll just be orienting yourself in your geo-temporal-spatial-spiritual landscape. This time is some of the most fun because it can be filled with unexpected and exciting experiences.

The fundamental exercise we'll use again is described in the chapter on decompositional magick, where we ventured out to make friends with a fungus. There might be little tweaks based on the type of spirit we're encountering, but to reiterate, the steps are: finding and assessing the being, opening communication, and making an offering if it's encouraged. Firstly, any collection you do should be legal. National and state parks often have strict prohibitions on collecting any species of plant or animal, rocks, water, and so on—in whole or in part. Secondly, if you're in a place not covered by these rules, make sure that collection is necessary and that you have gotten consent from any being whose bits you are collecting.

Spirit Allies:
Flora and Fauna

Spirits don't always take the form of what they look like to our eyes. As the spirit world is mutable, sometimes spirits will morph, change shape, or take on aspects of multiple parts of their life cycle simultaneously, and this is especially true of flora and fauna. Sometimes the spirit of a tree resembles a person, a glowing entity or orb, or a shade or shadow being. Working with more terrestrially slow species like plants, fungi, lichen, etc can be a little easier because once you find them, they tend to stay put and not run away.

Wildlife (including insects) are a little trickier to connect with, simply because they're more mobile and tend to want to quickly get the hell away from humans. But when you're working with animals, it's okay to go where you know they live. Visit a place where you've actually seen deer before, where you know a species of snake inhabits, or where you've found game trails that inform you that moose came through. When you do, just remember: be cautious.

If you visit a habitat that does have large animals (even if they're not predators, such as the lovely and sometimes terrifying moose), take necessary precautions. Don't be like those dopes who go to Yellowstone and try to pet the bison or feed the bears. Those are stupid people who have no real respect for the wild animals they're encountering. I promised myself I wouldn't say they deserve whatever they get, so I'll just stop there.

My point is that you can go out and make spirit contact with these beings without ever having seen them; in some instances, it's probably best that you don't see them unless you're in a well-protected space. You can commune with the spirit of tiger sharks without swimming with them, and that's okay.

Using Psychic Awareness

Open your psychic senses while you are venturing about and take note of any entities that you encounter. Sometimes they will actively move away from you, and sometimes you will want to get away from them. As mentioned earlier, some spirits have scared the hell out of me but more often those are land spirits, ancestral (human) spirits or spirits who have been created by human interaction and then abandoned. The nice part about working with any spirit is that you can call to them and ask them to be present, wherever you are. In a way, it belies the getting-out-in-nature part of the passionate screed that is this book but I do think it works better (and it's just more polite) to go to someone's house to introduce yourself when you want to hang out and be friends rather than demanding that they come to yours when you've never even spoken before. The connections where you encounter spirits in their home locations are also always more powerful in the same way that being closer to a cell tower gives you a better data connection.

Get out in nature, meet the spirit of the bunnies, and leave some offerings of water (or alcohol, if they are into it). If you find that you have things in common, such as being gentle, clever, and creative, you could start forging a friendship based on those commonalities. Or you could admire a quality in them like their quick wits when facing adversity that you'd like to bring into your energetic sphere. So you could praise them for those qualities and make offerings in the hopes of building a stronger relationship where they become a guide for you.

There are plenty of books that help you discern which plant or animal spirits you're encountering and what their common traits are, but if you're looking for some ideas (and you live in North America), some very common animal species people look to work with include rabbit, bear, wolf, rat, raccoon, opossum, beaver, woodchuck, bison, badger, wolverine, alligator, snakes, fish, manatee, otter, and weasels (and related family). Birds are numerous but the most commonly sought after by witches include raptos such as owls, hawks (and related species), eagles, and vultures; corvids such as crows, ravens, and jays; songbirds such as mockingbirds, robins, and finches, and water fowl such as ducks, herons, egrets, and storks. Plants include different kinds of sedges and grasses, marsh plants, trees native to your area, and so on. Look to local guides published for your bioregion to get even more ideas, and don't forget to rely on your instinct—listen to your psychic senses and work with whomever comes to you or you feel drawn to work with, especially if you don't know why they specifically appeared. For example, I've had the crow as a spirit guide since before I knew what spirit guides were. They are common enough but always seem to show up where I live, roosting in trees outside of my bedroom. I'm drawn to them, watching them wheel around in the air; I see them gathered in the trees chatting with each other and have buried more than a few after watching large numbers gather to swoop and call out over the body of a fallen comrade. I'll talk with them but generally don't offer them any food because I think it's unethical to offer food to a wild animal. But I will leave offerings of alcohol or blessed spring water to the spirit of crow.

Spirit Allies:
Land Wights

Land wights are a broad topic that deserve their own book. The important thing to remember is that I'm using the term "wight" as it is derived from old Norse practices because I think it more accurately captures more of what I mean when I refer to spirits of this type than any other word I've come across. I've adapted it for my own purposes and broadened it, but the overall character of what a wight is has been preserved.

In my definition, a land wight is any spirit of a place associated closely with that place and who characterizes one or more elements of place. Land wights are typically not mobile; if you move very far from where you currently live, you'll need to familiarize yourself with an entirely new set of spirits.

Land Wights and the Dead

One of the first things to know about land wights is that there is some overlap between them and the dead. There's even some overlap with old gods who have fallen out of human reverence or interaction. In my own experience, I've found that some human dead become less and less recognizably human over time and become more akin to unique spirits of place. This is especially true for human spirits who, in life, were particularly tied to a certain geographic area. It's also not very common that human spirits linger. While the godself returns to the source, the fetch self returns to the land, and the talker usually fades away. Traumatic events and injustices are the most common reason a spirit might become trapped in a specific place. The manny in which they become land spirits is either through an amalgamation of spirits trapped in a place over long periods of time or due to a sort of degradation of the personality and a lingering attachment to place. Again, it's complicated and difficult to understand. I might be entirely wrong in these assumptions but they are what was given to me as a reasoning for it from some of these entities themselves.

Mythology as a Resource

Other types of land wights include the various spirits that inhabit mythologies of people across the planet: the fair folk, dwarves, elves, sprites, will-o-wisps, trolls, goblins, orcs, ogres, giants, devils, giants, djinn—and yes, even old gods fit the bill.

As for angels and demons, they become nearly indistinguishable from each other the more you work with them, but are not in this general classification. Instead, they fall under a group of more primordial beings who represent and oversee some of the intrinsic processes of the universe.

The fair folk have a particularly Gaelic background that has informed the folklore of Gaelic speaking areas of the world. While I personally use the term "fae" or "faerie" to represent certain beings and practices I take part in, for the sake of this book it will stay connected to its home turf and to the Tuatha Dé Danann, the pre-Celtic gods and spirits associated with what is present-day Ireland and other parts of the Gaelic world. Dwarves and elves were similar spirits originating in areas generally inhabited by old Germanic tribes, and Scandinavian countries. Djinn are associated with areas of the Arabic world.

There are certain cultural differences that appear no matter where you are, but human interactions with non-human and also non-plant or animal spirits are common everywhere in the world. You could say that only in the modern world, have humans (generally) abandoned their communication and interaction with spirits, especially where the footprint of reason is felt as well as the specter of Christianity. This abandonment has led to a powerful degradation of how nature is viewed and valued and is greatly affecting how quickly we adapt to a rapidly changing world. We've got some fences to mend, and it's not going to be easy.

Be Cautious but Critical

For the most part, humans have been left baffled or terrified by their interactions with the land wight crew. After all, fairy tales and legends are rife with kidnapping us, taking us to elaborate courts, giving us food and drink, and then sending us home, where a hundred years have passed though we only experienced an adventure of an afternoon. Other stories also feature babies being swapped out for changelings, creatures disguised as our children who we are tricked into raising but have a sinister or strange quality about them. And in other stories, these beings wait until we're far from home and any help where they attack us and attempt to take our lives or everything that we own … or bake us into a pie … or turn us into animals. The checkmarks in the negatives column are pretty well stacked against our land wight friends. Maybe the age of reason is right and we are justified in abandoning these fraught relationships!

One counterpoint is the consideration that the authors of such stories are, to the best of our knowledge, human themselves. There might be a story somewhere about a cool stump to hide shiny things underneath written by a goblin, but for the most part it's all human authorship.

There might be some author biases against their odd and sometimes intimidating spirit world counterparts. What centuries of dualistic think-ing have imprinted upon much of Western thought is the notion that there are good and evil things in this world and that any variance from what one culture typifies as good means that an oppositional culture is simply evil. In countries like Iceland and Ireland, some of the old pre-Christian values still hold to this day; there are examples of modern people still attempting to honor agreements that have been made with the elves of Iceland, for exam-ple, by moving a planned road around rather than through a landmark com-monly believed to be their home.

We need to remember that every one of these spirits claims this earth as their home just as we do. Some of the spirits we encounter are the actual spir-its of a specific place such as a river, mountain, or forest. Some land wights can easily be found in your back yard if you know how to look for them, but some of the places to find them is in wild areas or areas that have been aban-doned and are in the process of rewilding. Think of areas around you that fit this description or areas that carry legends of oddity.

Another thing to consider: don't immediately negate areas that have rumors of cryptids (e.g., sasquatch, mothman, etc.) or UFO activity. There's an odd vein in modern witchcraft that is comfortable working with spirits, gods, and land wights to some extent, but the moment anything like cryptids or UFOs enter the picture, it becomes a bridge too far. Consider that such tales are essentially the modern-day equivalent of faerie or spirit sightings. The unexplained, then as now, is frequently and usefully couched within the framework that a person's cultural references allow for. Seeing a god float down from the heavens four hundred years ago spun in a modern-day mode of storytelling might take the form of a tale of a bright and erratic light that behaves in unexplainable ways. Part of the allure for many witchcraft practitioners is utilizing forces of nature that go beyond our current understanding of how our world works. In that pursuit of the unexplained and potentially beneficial, don't be so quick to write off some of the biggest troves of new information that could potentially help you in your pursuit because it sounds silly. Energy healing sounds silly, too, until you've seen it work.

Go exploring those areas that have their own legends and history. Maybe you'll make contact with a spirit that others have misunderstood, or maybe you'll find something that shifts your perspective. Landmarks or old monuments are great places to start looking. One of the best places I've ventured is an old landfill that has been restored to a park in the process of being restored and rewilded. There's a spirit there I eventually met but who had followed me around on many previous trips. I was able to make contact after persistently going back, setting out offerings, and waiting to see if they would approach. My persistence eventually paid off; I now have established a relationship with this being who helps me to better understand the working of magick in my area and how to use energy more effectively. The being has also shown me the unique way energy flows in this area.

Spirit Allies: The Dead

The last group of allies in this chapter are the dead. In many ways, the dead are the easiest to make contact with because, well, they used to be us! They know what it's like to be human and can more easily relate to our experiences. One of the best places to start in working with these allies is with your ancestral dead, the people responsible for your lineage, whose thoughts and opinions and actions have shaped who you are, what you believe, and how you see the world. This is true even of adopted family because you've been spiritually brought into the river of your adoptive family's lineage, something often called "the river of blood." If adoption is relevant to you, don't take what I say here as me writing off your background: think about the term "chosen family" and how much more powerful it can be—you were chosen to be added to a family line. They wanted you there and wanted to share their ancestral upbringing with you so much that they made it your own.

Start by becoming more familiar with your ancestral dead. If there are people in your family who know family history, start asking them about different family members and collecting stories. Try to get particular details that will help you reach out to them and make contact. Look for stories about how they met their partner, what they did for a living, their hobbies, or if they served in a war. What was their favorite song, food, cigarette brand if they smoked? Are there any family heirlooms or artifacts you might be able to acquire? On my family altar, I have a small embroidered handkerchief that belonged to my grandmother and serves as a touchpoint when I want to communicate with her and ask for guidance.

The Ancestral Burden of Trauma

Since this book focuses a lot on the process of healing to awaken our magick, there's another area to be discussed around the impact of ancestral trauma and how it is carried through generations. One of the most profound lessons I am still in the process of learning is forgiveness for the actions of the dead when living. Forgiveness can be incredibly difficult, especially if the person was abusive. You do *not* need to do this; if you're uncomfortable with even broaching the subject, please do what feels right for you.

For many years I had a name of someone in my family through which I had drawn a line in the book of names kept on my ancestral altar. On Samhain, I created a ritual for myself and my family to be freed from this person's abuse, which reverberated through the generations from my great grandfather to my grandfather, to my father, to me. When my child was born, I didn't want him to inherit that trauma and vowed to change the trauma response of my family heritage in order to free him. During this ritual, I crossed out this person's name and ritually abolished them from the family. As time has gone on, my practice with ancestors has deepened more and my feelings about that action have changed. Over time, I started to realize that the people I knew in life weren't quite the same in death, especially the longer they were separated from their lives. As I would reach out to them and make contact, their prejudices and idiosyncrasies seemed to fade or soften. It seemed that in death, they had a greater realization.

Because many in my family are Christian, I had feared even speaking to them would be considered a breach of their faith and that they would accuse me of necromancy (which it is) and want nothing to do with me. While some of them would most definitely have said that in life, I found that in death, the hard and fast rules of the living were kind of seen as superfluous or even ridiculous. While I had never been raised Christian, I was definitely brought up in a Christian culture, so this discovery really made me reconsider a lot of my assumptions. It was as that by being closer to whatever grand, unifying source underpins the universe, beliefs and prejudices had evaporated in death—and that includes anger and resentment.

The other people around the person I had so stridently decided to eliminate from the family legacy had forgiven him; amends had been made. That side of the veil doesn't work in the same way or on the same terms as this side. What was really challenging was even considering forgiving this person an aware father and spiritual worker; I could identify the trauma he had created and could see it cascading down through the generations—a tsunami that threatened to take down my family and bring us to ruin. Hard living, addiction, anxiety, depression, suicide, and serious physical ailments had plagued generation after generation from this individual's incitement: how could I be expected to follow the guidance of my ancestors and offer him forgiveness?

I was troubled for a long time, and the matter of forgiveness still troubles me every once in a while. However, the messages I kept getting from my beloved dead was that only the living carry the burden of what the living have done. The dead are free and in fact don't require our forgiveness at all. They tell me that if I want to heal the trauma of the bad he put into the world, then I had to heal myself and forgive the anger and hurt and everything else within me. It was hard to hear because it feels like there's no justice in it for the people who were hurt and had their lives destroyed. But the message reframed how I thought about what I'm carrying within myself. If it's true that harboring anger and hate for someone will negatively impact your life (and I believe it does), then the best thing for you is to let go of those resentments. Letting go may be one of the biggest lessons of my life, and I will probably not fully get it until I pass through the veil myself.

If this notion is disagreeable for you, I understand—it's still disagreeable for me sometimes. Letting go can bring up a lot of anger and unresolved emotions, but I view the work of the witch akin to the work of a monk in a lot of ways. It's as if this part of the work becomes alchemical: *solve et coagula* is the Latin phrase alchemists used to describe the process of dissolving or breaking things down—in this case, our complexes—and reforming into something stronger and healthier as a result of hard work. In alchemy, the goal is continuous refinement and removing impurities until lead is turned into gold. The metaphor is a wonderful focus for spiritual practitioners of any background who have a goal of eventual realization of their energies as part of the indistinguishable unity that is the cosmos.

The Deep Pool of Ancestry

Ancestors are typically thought of as the humans who came before us, our bloodline, or inherited bloodline. But consider that your life is a product of all evolution that led to you being here: the hominids, small furry mammals, reptiles, aquatic creatures, pools of algae, microbes—an uninterrupted line of reproduction and evolution that started with some amino acids in a pool of water and a strike of lightning. Even if you're an ardent atheist, when you look through the billions of years that have led to you, made of trillions of cells and about 8.5 octillion atoms (that's for a 150-pound adult; my atomic count is significantly higher—don't atom shame!) it is simply awe-inspiring.

Your atoms have been shared with other people, magma, kangaroos, bacteria and probably a couple popes which all resulted from an exploding star.[25] How anyone manages not to have their brains explode when thinking about it is probably a survival mechanism that evolved when early hominids came down from the trees, looked around at everything, and uttered those first, famous words: "holy fuuu—" before they fell over dead.

My point in bringing up evolutionary ancestry is don't be afraid to go wide and deep when you start working with ancestors. Ask the trees and lakes, the early primates, the microbial stew for guidance, inspiration, or whatever particular skill they have to aid you in the work of being a witch. Just like with art, the expressions are as infinite as the art you can make.

Working with Your Beloved Dead: A Practice

Without your ancestors, there wouldn't have been a you. If you start a family tree as an exercise of becoming more familiar with them, you'll quickly realize how unlikely your life is. Pull just one of those threads and you would never have existed, a fact that by itself is reason enough to honor those who have come before you.

If you want to work with your ancestors, you will need to set up a space in your home where you can commune with them. My personal ancestor altar is at an improvised hearth of my home. These days, fewer homes have fireplaces that fill the role of a true hearth; mine is on a bureau in the center of my home. When you visit, you are immediately confronted with what I now call "the family altar." On the right side is a wooden crate with pictures of my deceased family members in it. It's adorned with some family heirlooms, a crystal skull I use as a source for making contact with the dead, and some other accoutrements. There are no pictures of the living on it and no living people in any of the pictures with my ancestors, I received this guidance from others when I was first setting up my altar. While I don't remember the source, it's pretty much universal guidance at this point. I'm not entirely

---

25. Sarah Kaplan, "Dear Science: Could my body include an atom from Shakespeare?" *Washington Post*, December 27, 2016: https://www.washingtonpost.com/news/speaking-of-science/wp/2016/12/27/dear-science-could-my-body-include-an-atom-from-shakespeare/.

sure *why* it's the rule, but my suspicion has always been that there's a little bit of superstition as well as some practical reasons. On the superstition end, it seems like there's bad luck or bad energy in putting living people's representation on an altar made specifically for honoring the dead. The practical argument flows from that: it's a space for honoring your dead kin, so mixing in living people is inappropriate and energetically misaligned.

If you don't have pictures of family members or are working to get them but want to get started, you can keep it very simple. You can even set up a temporary altar space at your kitchen table that you can break down after doing the work if you like. It's best to work toward making something permanent because family being family, they'll likely want to drop in at unexpected times and will need a space that's comfortable to do so. You can't just go knocking your bills off the table every time they need a place to sit!

Make some coffee or pour them their favorite drink. You could even offer water, just to offer them something. Also set out some food; a favorite treat is great, but some cookies, a peanut butter and jelly sandwich, or a bowl of nuts will work if you don't have their faves. On my permanent altar, I leave a clean glass of water, some cornmeal, and a candle that I leave burning from morning until bedtime, battery-operated nowadays because my wife got tired of soot stains around the house from all the candles I had going. It was like a church around here. Now it's just like a church with cleaner air.

I'll leave out more substantial food on special occasions, but I always make sure to remove everything at the end of the day and dispose of it off of my property. Sundays are family days around my home, and that extends to my ancestors as well. That's usually the day I'll dump the water and cornmeal outside and wash and refresh everything.

Exercise
Contacting Your Beloved Dead

Dim the lights, set out your coffee or drink and food offerings, and light a candle. Do the candle flame exercise, feeding the flame with the energy gathered in the earth and stellar darkness meditation. Sit quietly for a while. Let your mind and body relax, pull errant thoughts back, and focus on the flame burning in your heart space and in front of you. See them meld together and close your eyes. Feel your heart thumping in your chest as it moves your blood through your body, blood that is tied to your ancestors through birth or choice, the blood that flows through you connecting you to them. In your mind's eye see that blood flowing back and back and back through time. Back through all of the uncountable generations that link you together. Hundreds, thousands and more people all with a vested interest in your well-being, who want you to succeed because your success is their success.

Breathe gently and stay connected with your heartbeat. Feel the rhythm of life and know that this rhythm connects you to all of humanity. When it stops, you will be an ancestor helping from the other side, just as your ancestors are doing now. But today, you are making contact and seeking a message. From the countless shadows who stand before you, one you may recognize moves forward and takes a seat at the table across from you. Take a moment to see them, sometimes the veil makes it difficult. If you don't know them well or never met them in life, take a moment to ask their name and how you might be connected. If you recognize them, start to talk with them, remembering that your psychic method of communication may require you to receive messages in different ways. Stay open and receptive, and try to remember what you've been told or take notes if needed.

When you've finished speaking with your beloved dead, say, "Thank you for your presence. I bless and release you." It's important to keep it to just one visitor for a while, you may find that there are others who are lining up and eager to get your attention. You can gently let them know that they'll have an opportunity to speak with you in the future or simply tell them that you can't speak today. It's very important to pull back any energies you were expending while you were in your trancelike state and to ground out any energy so that you can fully and completely return to normal consciousness. As always, eat or drink something to help with the process if needed.

Any offerings that you have given to the beloved dead need to be moved off of your property and disposed of, including coffee, cookies, etc. Don't forget and absentmindedly start munching on snacks you left out for grandma!

This work can get very emotional, especially if you receive messages from someone with whom you were very close. It was that way for me with a family member for a while after they passed but I've grown so accustomed to being able to communicate with them now that it's as if they're always here, like calling them on the phone. And eventually that's what it sort of turns into: you can light a candle and ask for their advice, request healing energy from the other side, and even do things that they left unfinished. I don't frequently get asked to finish their business, because as I've stated before, they're moving on a different level where what they consider important is different from what we consider important.

Other Work with the Dead

You may decide that you need to employ the help of someone outside of your family lineage. This is where your knowledge and research into local history will help out! Finding out who historically lived in your area and where they're buried can offer great opportunities.

Judges, politicians, the wealthy, inventors, artists and more can be excellent resources for you. For example, lots of people turn to judges for favor if they're in a legal bind, or to successful real estate magnates for help finding a new home. You don't have to necessarily like these people in order to work with them (after all, how many of your coworkers do you really like?) but you can still work together to accomplish your goal.

Historical cemeteries are some of the best places to visit because they're sometimes well-tended by historical societies who recorded biographical details and easy-to-follow directions to where the person in question is buried. So if you need help for a family member who is sick, knowing where the doctor who discovered a cure for an infectious disease is buried would be really helpful.

There are some things to keep in mind when you're doing this work. Firstly, entering a cemetery as a spirit worker is a little different than taking a stroll. Most spirit workers leave a coin at the entrance, traditionally a Mercury head dime. These have grown increasingly hard to find and are thus expensive, so any coin will do. In a nod to tradition, I try to stick with dimes. What you are effectively doing when you leave a coin is buying your way into the realm of the dead and ensuring that you'll be able to leave with what you entered with (i.e., your life) when the time comes.

When you come to the threshold of the cemetery, put the coin down on the fence or just over the barrier. If you work with any cthonic (underworld or death) deities, ask that they give you safe passage and protect you until your work is done. If you don't, you can ask that the keeper of the cemetery grant you entry and make a promise that feels suitable for you, e.g., "I vow to honor those who rest here and will try not to disturb anyone too much." Be vague with any promises you make because if you break them, you'll probably want to leave very quickly.

The next thing to keep in mind is what to bring as an offering. Flowers are of course quite common; some people bring bottles of alcohol, but some of that old standby water, especially spring water, will work just as well. Some cemeteries have adopted littering rules where they discourage people from leaving offerings at grave sites, which makes a little alcohol or water that can be poured out an even better choice.

Finally, bring something for the dead to place their energetic signature on, such as a candle you intend to burn as part of a spell or some other physical object.

Some people like to collect things when they go to a cemetery—please don't do that. Not only is it unethical, but it's also nearly universally illegal and usually punishable as a grave robbing offense, something few (living) judges have sympathy for. Remember that you're at someone's family member's grave site: be honorable in your intentions and actions. You're here to conduct business between you and the spirit, but they have families and are someone's ancestor too.

When you find the grave of the person you want to work with, stop and take a few moments to connect with them. Lay a hand on their gravestone or marker and feel if they're active. More well-known dead are usually visited more often, which keeps the energy more alive if you'll forgive the poor turn of phrase. If the grave is still, you could try offering something and see if you get a reaction but if you're not getting anything after that, it's best to move on.

When you do find an active grave site, try reaching out and seeing if they're receptive. If they are, you can proceed and let them know the nature of your request, tell them about your court case, your sick family member and what you hope they could do for you. Let them know about the offering that you're willing to give them in exchange and see if they assent. If they do, pour out or place the offering and then lay down the candle or whatever else you want them to imbue with their energy on top of their grave. When you feel it's charged with their energy, remove it and thank them before departing, but don't make a big production out of it, either. You've entered into essentially what is a business transaction and should keep it professional.

Over time you may develop a deeper relationship with different spirits met in this way, especially if they resonate deeply with some part of your professional or personal life.

Are All Spirits Guides or Allies?

One thing to take away from everything you've read thus far is that the world is filled with spirits: there are spirits of individual beings and the overspirit that manifests them all. Spirits on spirits on spirit—we're never truly alone. Are all the spirits we meet guides or allies? It might seem a silly question at first; after all, are all humans your friends? Are all dogs eager to be your buddy? I don't think it's silly at all. When you're new to interacting with the spiritual realm, every encounter offers an opportunity to learn. Are the spirits you encounter your best friends? Do they even have your best interest in mind? Definitely not, but in a sense any interaction offers guidance, even if that guidance is to stay away from this big meanie. Should you refer to them as your guide? Probably not, just like you wouldn't necessarily call a professor who gave you a failing grade in a class a mentor. The difference is that, just like with a mentor, your relationship with a spirit guide should be based on mutual trust and an understanding of clear boundaries.

9.
Time

On a late Tuesday morning in May, I was listening to ambient music and snowfall in my south Florida home. This soundscape, muted, gentle, dreamy has become an important backdrop to my experience of writing. Every day I put energy into the spell that is the working of this book. It is its own ritual, and that's why I know that it will find completion and success. On my desk, a steaming mug of herbal tea—anise, fennel, cardamom, licorice, coriander, turmeric harvested months ago and a continent away—weave their way into my words giving luck, power, communication, and poise. I offer thanks to their spirits for their sacrifice which has enriched me. Where and when all of these circumstances and spirits came together was not a matter of *if* it would happen, it always would.

Time and space are inextricably linked, and the place and time in which this book was written reflect that fact. It's a resonance from one part of the world from one point in time and one person's perspective. To an almost universal extent, we have agreed to live our lives based on the calculations that have been accepted as the parsing out of a single revolution of our planet before it returns to roughly the same locale. Our days are not as rigid as we'd like them to be, however, so every four years we add a day to catch up for lost time. It's an interesting concept, catching up to something that we as a species have tried so hard to make a universal truth, and it's worked out for the most part.

It does make you wonder if it's so universal, why haven't we adapted our systems to real time instead of manufactured time? Writing for *Noēma* magazine, Joe Zadeh says:

> *Clock time is not what most people think it is. It is not a transparent reflection of some sort of true and absolute time that scientists are monitoring. It was created, and it is frequently altered and adjusted to fit social and political purposes. Daylight saving, for instance, is an arbitrary thing we made up. So is the seven-day week.*[26]

Technology and Time

While the trains, buses, and planes rarely arrive on time, we know that they are early or late because that's what our phones (which manage time via satellites orbiting Earth) tell us. With the help of electricity and a universally managed clock, we are able to conduct business almost unimpeded by our body's natural, hormonal clocks which respond to sunrise and sunset. The Nap Ministry has a lot of useful messages around reclaiming yourself from clock time, especially for Black Americans. Just be warned, Tricia Hersey's truths are razor sharp and as accurate as an Olympic archer.

Have you noticed how time keeps speeding up the more exposure you have to technology? Now that the lay person can easily account for time down to the thousandths of a second using an app on their phone, it means that all time can be accounted for. If you're like most people, you punch a clock that used to measure down to minutes. Now it takes into account seconds. I've been chastised by a boss in the past for being a minute late, but have you ever been reprimanded for being a second late? Expect it, because it's coming. Beyond the labor aspects, how much are you able to focus your attention? Can you sit quietly with one task for twenty minutes without checking your phone? Most people now can't, and it's by design. The little interruptions from your mobile device are like mosquitos draining you dry one notification

---

26. Joe Zadeh, "The Tyranny of Time" *Noēma*, June 3, 2021, https://www.noemamag.com /the-tyranny-of-time/. Noēma Magazine is an extension of the Berggruen Institute, which has as a few of its pillars, sustaining capitalism and moving us toward a future of human genetic engineering and climate engineering. They're not on my personal besties list, but this article is good at digging into the problems of time and how it creates discontents.

at a time. And as your mind becomes more fragmented, the demands grow so much that maintaining a social media account becomes an unpaid job. How much time do you think you have available after that?

There's much to be said about the speed of information transfer. A generation ago, we would hear about world events via television, before that, radio and prior to that, newsprint on paper. The rapidity and volume of news stories a person can be exposed to in an hour dwarfs what the average newspaper reader could consume in a full sitting and reading the daily press. Our brains aren't designed to handle or process this much information, something that is fairly obvious when we step back and see that our peers, parents, and even cities and nations are behaving quite a bit more erratically than even a dozen years ago. Time as a concept is becoming compressed as we witness the full spectacle of human tragedy unfold before us in real time. The only reaction that people have to it anymore is to either shut down or wade in and deliver their own hot takes, the social currency of the moment. If you feel anxious, scattered, or like you're barely able to keep it together, you're not alone. This is what compressing and fragmenting time does to your brain!

The late philosopher and thinker, Alan Watts, reflected on the sacrifice of cohesive thought on the altar of technology:

> *The miracles of technology cause us to live in a hectic, clockwork world that does violence to human biology, enabling us to do nothing but pursue the future faster and faster. Deliberate thought finds itself unable to control the upsurge of the beast in man—a beast more "beastly" than any creature of the wild, maddened and exasperated by the pursuit of illusions. Specialization in verbiage, classification, and mechanized thinking has put man out of touch with many of the marvelous powers of "instinct" which govern his body. It has, furthermore, made him feel utterly separate from the universe and his own "me."* [27]

At the very least, we can start with establishing an awareness of our technology use. The "beast" Watts mentions above is frequently within our

---

27. Alan Watts, *The Wisdom of Insecurity: A Message for an Age of Anxiety* (New York: Vintage Books, 1951), 52.

desires, compulsions, personality, and presence in the world. The illusion that the metaverse is real and worthy of our attention. It may feel like it is until we're not part of it anymore; once we leave, we realize how trifling a thing it is. But you have to be comfortable interacting on a more compressed scale.

Universality of Time

But what if we take a stab at the universality of things? Knowing that it's nearly impossible to dictate the terms of your life without being part of time, what if you spent more of your conscious existence in true universal time? Ritual time? Time that surges and lags, dawdles and lunges? There's a linearity to the arrival of the tea on my desk, a chain of events that brought it to me. There's also the experience of connecting with its spirit and bioregion. It's probably possible to grow many of the herbs in this tea where I live, but it's also not the case that it happened that way. To connect with their spirits is, in a sense, to step outside of time. The herbs are not objects but subjects; they are alive and possessed with their own unique signature no other thing in the universe has. This is what working with spirit time begins to uncover.

The ritual of my gratitude is a near daily occurrence that has happened countless times and sets forth its own resonance. That it ever occurred means in some very minute way, it is an event that will always be and always was a part of the universe. It might seem like heady stuff for a book like this or for where you are in your practice but it's an important factor to entering liminal space. The liminal isn't outside of time, it is *all* of time. Does magick require a deep understanding of just how mutable and warped time is for it to work? Definitely not, but it will greatly alter the way you conceive of your workings and guide you through ethical dilemmas that you have along the way. If you are prepared to move a working from out of your own mind and make it live—eternally—in the universe whether a blessing or a curse, then may the gods light your way. You start to get a real idea of why some Jainist monks are so exacting about moving through the world and doing as little harm as possible, to the extent that they wear mesh in front of their faces and sweep paths as they walk to avoid harming insects. When your actions potentially harm life and those actions are crystalized as part of the all that is, was and ever will be, it's a real responsibility!

A Note About Pacts, Spiritual and Otherwise

The slippery slope of sensing your actions as they relate to karma should be pretty obvious by now, I hope. While karma is not a part of my beliefs or practice, something akin to it is there, borne from this mindset.

Before you throw yourself at the first goddess who winks your way, sign a pact or make an agreement, just remember that its resonance will be there always. Even if it doesn't work out later and you are able to part ways on good terms, the action of joining oneself to that spirit is there. It will be a part of your story and the story of the universe.

This is Not Classical Moralism

There is no reckoning other than the reckoning with yourself. If your worldview includes a hell, adjust accordingly; mine does not. Cussing at other drivers on the highway is still a part of my regular experience but one that I'm trying to improve on for my own personal growth and because I don't want to be that person (trust me, Florida drivers will try you). An important distinction here is that there is also no "have to" in this. If I'm perfectly okay with being the type of person who flies into a rage whenever a teenager in a $350,000 sports car flies across six lanes of traffic to cut me off, I am fully empowered to be that person. Likewise, if I reasonably believe that cursing someone is justified in my own mind given whatever circumstances, I'm free to curse away. The ramifications are more upon reflection, something that seems to empowers sociopaths, though I'm *also* free to take action against sociopaths. And the wheel keeps turning.

Doesn't This Mean That There is No Free Will?

One of the issues that sometimes arises with the idea of time being a nonlinear construct appears as the next easy leap in logic: do any of us have free will since everything is happening at once or has already happened? This is one of the great mysteries for which there are no real answers—it could be the case … or not, or both at the same time, or hundreds of other combinations of yes, no, maybe so. We'll probably never know. In Robert Jordan's *Wheel of Time* series, the "wheel" of the title spins threads woven into the fabric of time, but the pattern laid down is dependent on how each of the people (the threads of the fabric), decide what actions to take in different circumstances. The fabric is inescapable, but the threads within the pattern have the freedom to move anywhere (something that holds true over multiple lifetimes) as long as they don't leave the fabric. It's an imperfect metaphor—there is still a sense of linearity to the process—but it's another way of thinking about it.

Things get very esoteric very quickly. but there are plenty of examples of cultures and peoples who live with nonlinearity as part of their experience of life. It's safe to say that the version of time we live with is not the only by far.

The Greatest System that Needs to be Upended Lives Within You

It becomes comfortable to rail against a system that has broken personal freedom, stolen your natural biological impulses, turned you into a slave to the clock, but that's only half of the story. Externalizing and expelling the mindset that has been engrained from almost the beginning of your life is on you because there are no Imagineers around to assist you out of the park when you don't like the ride anymore. That system is yours for the breaking, but it's a hard row to hoe. Most people decide that they're better off staying in it. But there are half-measures that can be taken; it's not all-or-nothing, and in some cases it's a matter of gradual progress.

So how do you begin to break down a system that our phones, computers, bosses, and families all use, a system that we collectively and unthinkingly obey? One of my favorite news articles in recent years was about a Norwegian town that declared they were no longer part of clock time and would no longer adhere to working or living by its constraints.[28] While it was revealed that the town had created a partnership with the national tourism

---

28. Anna Schaverien, "Living Life by the Clock? Norwegian Island Wants to Go 'Time Free,'" *New York Times*, June 26, 2019, https://www.nytimes.com/2019/06/26/world/europe/norway-time-free-island.html.

board, the mayor and many of the people involved later insisted it wasn't a stunt. Because of their position north of the Arctic circle, they enjoy endless daylight for almost half of the year, earning the name *Sommaroy* or "Summer Island." People who live there are exposed to so much daylight that they don't have a strong adherence to what the clock means anymore. There are a few businesses, like a local hotel that still do because they need to know when guests need to check out, but for the most part at all times of day, you're likely to see people out walking, playing soccer, or picnicking. It's not exactly the same as living independent of time; their bodies will obviously age and eventually die, but it's an interesting option for how humans can live that seems refreshing when compared to how most of the rest of us are forced to live. It's hard to uncrack an egg, but there are ways to reclaim your time, the biggest of which is to step outside it or stretch it out, which is what we'll do in the next exercise.

Clock time was created mostly to organize labor, and the first step to unwinding it is to reclaim parts of your labor as your own. At the time of this writing, we're in the midst of what's been dubbed the Great Resignation, but it's more accurate to say that we're waking up from resignation to reclaim our lives.

Wages have not kept up with the cost of living and in fact have spiraled downward. People are working more and making less than their parents did while the prices of everything have increased. And the matter of the pandemic has everyone rethinking their priorities.

There's no advice I can give you other than to follow your heart and your best interest, however you define it. We live in strange times, an axiom that's eternally true.

The zeitgeist of this moment offers some interesting magickal possibilities and revolves around the idea of reclaiming. Large systems require willing participants to continue working. Business, manufacturing, retail—all require at least moderately productive workers in order to keep making money. The less productive we collectively are, the more power we begin to have.

Most thinking people at this point in time are against the concept of colonization, seeing it for what it is: a system of theft often perpetrated under the most racist beliefs possible, wherein the colonized as somehow less human because the (historically, frequently European) colonizers couldn't or didn't want to be bothered with trying to comprehend the cultures of the colonized. Colonization became capitalism, and the act of colonization never stopped, it just turned to colonizing our minds, dreams, and imaginations.

Say you have a passion, any passion in the world that you do purely for the love of it—painting or drag racing or cheese making. How many times have you heard from someone, "oh, you could make money doing that? Why don't you sell it?" How many times have you yourself followed that same line of thinking? The moment you start to take a little bit of joy in anything, you think, "How can I turn this into a job?" This line of questioning is the inescapable sickness we're all party to, and one of the best things you can do is try to put a wall around it and protect the sanctity of your own joy with your life. To do things just for the simple pleasure of it is courageous, challenging, and a thumb in the eye of the rapacious system we live in. And while it is nearly impossible to live in this culture without adhering to a good number of its ideals, the more areas that can still be cordoned off and kept sacrosanct, the better.

"Easy for the guy writing a book on witchcraft to say," you think, and I agree: what we live under makes heretics and deceivers of us all. At no point is it easy to say no and be able to stick to it. Two points on the writing books thing though: there's only one James Patterson, Stephen King, and Mary Higgins Clark, and more than 99 percent of authors don't make a living off their trades and can't pay a month's rent from what they make in a year or five. Everyone's got bills to pay and we do what we need to stay in the black as much as we can. But consider this: there is freedom beyond the dumb, materialist approach to the world.

Even in total poverty, yoked to the system and without a seeming breath for a clear thought, you can find it and once you tune into it, it becomes expansive. I've been evicted, unemployed, employed but still in poverty; I've starved, lived off of shift meals at restaurants, and let's not forget that bag of almonds that eked me through a summer. I've lived off of dumpster diving and found a huge score of fresh food thrown in the trash only to experience the heartbreak that the store had poured boxes of powdered bleach over all of the food. I've used hospitals as my main and only form of health-care and had to wait the seven years for those collections to fall off of my report before I could attempt to rebuild my life. I'm not saying all of this to get any sort of poverty cred, I'm saying it to relay that I've been there and also recognize that other people have suffered much worse. But rethinking my approach to how time feels allowed me to change my relationship with myself in a way that wasn't possible before. It softened my anger and helped steer me toward a deeper resolve. That, in turn, allowed me to conceptualize ways out of my circumstances and not feel so bound to a system that was not benefiting me or my health in any way.

Exercise
Stopping Linear Time

This exercise is about altering our experience of time from something linear to something nonlinear or, at the very least, non-present in a deeper meditative state. Start with the aligning exercise and follow it with the world earth and stellar darkness meditation.

Now I want you to start thinking about time as a stream of successive moments flowing from the past and into the future. Everyone has the general sense that there's a before, a now, and an after or future. People use metaphors such as "time is a river." Think of that river flowing away in front of you, feeding you from behind. The water is time itself and you are along for the journey, floating contentedly but unable to battle the current that carries you along.

As you reflect, think of times where that river has been peace-ful, slow moving, and expansive. These are some of the happier memories, some of the good moments in life. You can also reflect on times where the river has been swift and violent, where you've felt tossed about, nearly incapable of staying afloat. These are obvi-ously the challenges, tragedies, and traumas you've experienced.

Where on this river are you right now? Somewhere between these extremes? Somewhere you want to be or don't want to be?

Take a moment and see the river shift: rather than you floating on it, begin to see it flowing through you, maybe directly from your heart space, each moment an effervescent bubble, like soda water poured into a glass, like a candle flickering this way and that in a light draft. There's a fount of is-ness flowing from you now, no past to reflect on, no future to worry about. Just this moment. And this moment. And this moment right now. Sit with this feeling. As with meditation, when thoughts of the past or the future creep in, gently set them aside and focus on the bubble of this moment, the flick of the flame at this second. There is only you right now, and in your aloneness you find a connection with all that is. Think to yourself, "this moment is perfect, this moment is pure, there is nothing other than this moment." Settle your consciousness here, in a place that is similar to the no-thought goal of the Buddhists. In this place, embrace every point of consciousness in the universe and judge them not at all. Time now can be seen as that consciousness, another aspect for determining location within space and nothing more. In this experience, you might find something that feels like a looseness in the foundations you're standing on. The "I" of who you are can begin dissolving in this state as you begin seeing the consciousness of the entirety of being as the same thing.

When you have sat with this experience for an adequate amount of time, gently allow yourself to step out of this state and back to your more linear consciousness. Settle yourself. If you feel out of sorts or discombobulated by the ride, take some extra time to reorient yourself within your body. It's a generally good idea to do the grounding exercise. Eat some food, move your body around, or do whatever will help you feel more tuned into your surroundings.

Journal about your experience and any thoughts that arise when you reflect on what the experience meant for you.

To some people, this exercise will feel identical to meditation. For others, there will be a subtle difference. It really depends on your personal experience and what you've learned on your path or how you've been taught.

When I was going through one of the roughest patches of my life, I started doing walking meditations on my way to my job. I didn't own a car, my bike had been stolen, and public transportation was very limited, so there were occasions where I would have to walk as much as six miles to and from work. That much walking through a city can be boring or disheartening, especially if there's a job waiting at the end that you're not too thrilled about. This was also when smartphones as we know them today didn't exist. iPods were new and so expensive that you'd get robbed for them. I had been reading and learning about meditation for some time and decided that a walking meditation was the best way to spend that time. And I spent that time by stepping outside of time, just like the meditation above. The benefits it offered was surprising—I showed up to work feeling mentally fresh and like I had just left my house rather than the hour-plus I had left earlier.

Try incorporating this exercise into any repetitive physical activity such as jogging or walking and see how far it gets you. When you're ready, move on to the next exercise.

Navigating Time

As stated earlier, one of the greatest systems that needs to be upended lives within you. Especially today in the information overload we experience through our phones, it's easy to come away from our day feeling like it was jam-packed full and that we can never unplug. The reality is that no one *does* unplug anymore. While we're all out there hustling to earn money, we're also gorging our brains on the emptiness of social media, celebrities, and whatever outrage we are personally attuned to. It is costing all of us our lives because we are in a constant state of being plugged in.

Taking a walk? Better get a selfie. Stopped for a coffee? Better take a pic of your drink with a shout-out to your favorite barista. Trying on a shirt? Better DM your bestie to get their feedback. When you examine your day, how many moments did you have in which you were present with yourself without documenting what was happening and sharing it with others? This exercise goes hand in hand with the previous one. In contrast to the last exercise, which covered time in nonlinear fashion, this exercise will be about putting your phone away and being bored.

For your mind to get into a state that allows for creative thought, you must feed it with...nothing. Your brain appreciates the challenge of lacking stimulus and begins inventing its own things to occupy itself. It's in the daydream state that feels so similar to the state of mind you're in as you drift off to sleep. Your brain starts making up stories and before you know it, you're asleep and you've used a set of pliers to remove the wings from a golden lion statue that is somehow linked to your childhood best friend's mother.

In this state, artists and writers find their best inspiration. And as was covered in the chapter on healing, we should use this state to create our healing art. So here's the exercise: put down your phone. Put down this book. Sit quietly for an hour until you feel really bored.

"Wait a minute," you're thinking, "isn't this a book on witchcraft?" You bet it is. One of the best ways to become a badass witch who lives the craft is challenging yourself to see differently from everyone else. When society is telling everyone to look in one direction, it's the witch's work to look everywhere else to see what's really going on. The most transformative acts happen when you ask why, when you try to experience something that isn't easy or try to do something that's free.

Try setting a timer for an hour and then attempt to do literally nothing—no phone, no books, no streaming, just sitting. It won't take very long before your brain is screaming for the dopamine hit your phone gives it or until you've almost said "to hell with it" and check your phone a dozen times. And when that alarm finally sounds off, see if you're not in the middle of planning a vacation, plotting out a book, or conceptualizing a piece of art. Congratulations, you've just reclaimed time and a small part of yourself by embracing boredom.

Our world is so geared around productivity and *maximizing* every moment that the simple act of sitting is quite nearly a magickal act of its own. Stop trying to be the person out there killing it, and start reclaiming your humanity.

We're going to combine some of what we've practiced, taking the time exercise from this chapter and the small death exercise from the chapter on rewilding your souls and putting them together. Grab a palm stone or something similarly sized to hold in your hand. Whatever you pick should have a little weight to it because you'll be using as a device to bring you back to your physical body after the working. If you like, you can also set a timer or alarm for when you want to return from your experience; ten to fifteen minutes should be enough.

Exercise
The Vehicle of Time

Once again, do the aligning exercise and the earth and stellar darkness meditation. Get yourself as relaxed as possible and revisit that flowing stream of time, the river that moves you along with or without your input. You are bobbing along on this current, and now you'll begin unplug your thoughts from past and future, where all that exists is this moment right now.

And this one.

And this one.

Each moment is like a little bubble popping on the surface.

You aren't in the past or future; you have no past or future; you are just at this moment, which is the same as all eternity.

Expand, expand, expand. Reach to every corner of the universe with a breath. All points are accessible to you: the birth of the universe, your own birth, the birth of your child or someone dear to you, the death of the universe, your own death, the death of your child or someone dear to you, and all the forms and permutations that have taken place in every moment.

When you have achieved presence and begin to feel the scattered nonlinear expanse of everything that is, breathe it all in—breathe in every point of light, every galaxy in the billions, every uncountable star and every dimension where all beings dwell.

Now exhale, sending all of it back. The cosmic eruption and enfolding, enacted in a single breath.

With each intake of breath, you become more expansive and realize that you're not actually taking any of it into yourself; rather, you've learned to scatter your consciousness across it all, and the *you* has fallen away, having connected to the conscious field that is elemental to the universe.

This presence yawns and stretches and becomes the great orgasm of birth-life-death-rebirth. In this state, time does not exist. Sit with this experience.

Now, slowly and carefully, begin to call all the disparate parts of yourself back. Feel the weight of the palm stone (or whatever you decided to use) in your hand.

Recite this charm:

A finger wrapped in ribbon,
Stars gather, cluster near,
A gentle kiss at dawn,
The threads spool back and clear

The more experience you have doing this work, the easier it becomes. What's interesting is that it also becomes easier to recall the sense of timelessness it creates and bring it into your everyday life. This ability is what I would call the activated presence of the true state of time. At first it seems metaphorical but as with many magickal things, it ends up creating its own presence in your day-to-day that you will find invaluable.

One of the more interesting things I've been able to do while experimenting with this technique is combine it with spellwork. See if you can make time slow down if you need more time to study or do another task that requires focus and a consuming attention. Conversely, see if you can speed up a slow day at work that drags and drags. Setting an intention that two minutes will pass as one, for example, might find you at the end of the day with enough energy to enjoy time with friends instead of simply crashing on the couch.

The final part I'll brush lightly upon because it requires more active exploring and much more advanced work than can be covered here. At some point you'll realize that what you've created is almost a vehicle for travel to other times or realms, a way to make contact with ancestors and glean their wisdom, or a way to visit with the gods and seek direction. I'm not getting too much into how to do this part because there's a level of discernment that needs to be cultivated before you're ready to make that journey. Being able to tell if what you're experiencing is real or just really what you want to hear is a critical skill that sometimes even the most experienced get wrapped up with.

Another important and potentially hazardous area is getting into using this technique for divination or scrying. Suffice it to say this exercise is a clearly off-label application; you're better off sticking to using it for its intended purpose.

Concerning the vehicle concept, it was many years afterwards that I found a likeness in the description of the merkabah of Jewish mysticism. In brief, the merkabah is a meditative tool used to travel between the realms, through time, and more deeply into oneself. It is quite similar to what we've been doing in this chapter and worth digging into more deeply if you're interested in going to the next level with this work.

Time Magick

There are many ways to approach the working of time magick, but I will say that as oddly phrased as some of the work in this chapter may seem, it becomes more and more familiar when you begin practicing it. Think of the first time you ever drove a car and how foreign it all felt. Accounting for all the extra space that cars occupy is strange and intimidating; the gas pedal doesn't work as you expect it to, and the brakes are way too aggressive. Then you have to steer the whole mess on top of it! But in no time at all, it starts to feel like an extension of yourself. You gain spatial awareness that (for most drivers) extends to the boundaries of your car, and you're able to drive without actively thinking about it all that much or at least nowhere near the amount of awareness put into it when you first turned the key in the ignition.

Sensing fields of consciousness is similar to your ability to feel the amount of space your vehicle is occupying, even though you aren't yourself a vehicle. Tapping into that field is an odd and tentative process at first, but then you begin to understand that consciousness is a feature of the universe and that our brains are basically translating the field of consciousness into our lived experience. When everything is conscious, it really does change your relationship with everything else. This is where we start getting into personhood and subjectivity as the default mode rather than materialist objectivity where the universe is simply filled with objects that can be manipulated. And now we've gotten into how time, space and consciousness are all inseparable. Whoops! This is what happens when you ask too many why questions in a witchcraft setting! You start out with some statues and a candle and the next thing you know, field theory!

Cultivate more of it for yourself, live outside of it, do parlor tricks to impress your friends and neighbors! Enjoy the wild, surreal beauty that is living in this universe. Also your boss probably expects too much of you and you should take an extra break.

10.

The Gate at the Edge
of the Garden

My witchcraft began with a single spark—the first magickal act was lighting a match and watching it explode into life and then gently transferring that flame to a candle. It was like watching the universe being born and, in a sense, it was for me that day. From that moment on, I knew that the immanence of spirit in our world was a fact, not just some philosophical exercise. Lighting a match and bringing the life of the flame to a candle wick was my first hedge riding experience. I was transported somewhere else, given keys to a kingdom I had only visited in my early youth.

There's something about the candle, the flame, that captures your awareness. Fire can be deadly; it is a creature that only knows consumption, craving more, lusting to be fed until there's nothing left. And yet it's also a powerful ally. Cooking food has allowed *Homo sapiens* to unlock nutrients from vegetables, grains, fruit, and meat that we wouldn't have otherwise had access to. Cooking kills pathogens and breaks down materials into forms our digestive systems can handle.

Fire also illuminates the night, stretching our ability to make use of hours that would normally have been lost to sleep. It protects us by chasing away predators who have a healthy fear of fire. In so many ways, fire has been vital to our evolution. We hunted in vast grasslands for hundreds of thousands of years, developed smarter ways to catch prey, cooperated for the health and sustainability of all and then we were able to transcend it all and leapfrog our own evolution by discovering how to reliably create fire.

Every time you light a candle, you call back to those earliest days—perhaps this is why we are still transfixed by a fire when we're near one. Staring into the embers and watching the flames flit about, we're transported to those earliest days of comfort, food, and community sustained by fire. We cross the hedge into an early version of who we are as a species and discover that we're not all that different, in spite of the passage of millennia.

Just a Candle

Some practices throw you into the deep end. There's value in that, but it can also be dangerous. It's a method better suited for in-person training and really only appropriate for certain people. For the work of this book, you'll start by meditating on a candle.

When I was growing up, oh so many years ago, there was a lot of detritus from the '70s, the sort of collected cultural materia that ended up being transported through time without context to be puzzled over by succeeding generations. Among all the prized dross I claimed there was a candle made to look as if it was composed of rock. The candle had red wax seeping out between the cracks, giving the impression of something seen on a volcanic island far out in the Pacific. Along with a pair of carved wooden figurines that slightly resembled Easter Island moai statues, I had the makings of my first altar. There was even some grotesque Money House Blessing brand incense, the one with the horrifically racist Native American logo, in strawberry. All these distasteful elements aside, I learned about a connection to something that I hadn't even identified having a need for. The act of turning off the lights, burning incense, and lighting a candle was so transformative, it was like crawling through the back of a wardrobe and discovering a whole new world. Because I had such a strong connection to the fantasy genre, it felt like I was taking the first step toward actualizing the feelings and yearning that reading about powerful worlds of magick, gods, monsters, and more created in my young psyche.

As the first step on our journey in crossing the threshold of what is perceived as the normal or mundane world, we'll perform the simple act of candle gazing to summon the spirit of fascination and awe.

Find a good candle and some matches. On my spiritual path, that's a tall, black pillar candle. Some folks follow different paths in the craft that use more than one, but we'll stick to a single candle for now as we focus our work and prepare for journey work. Use whatever color appeals to your sense of magick and mystery. It's fine if you'd like to have incense, but make sure it's not strawberry!

Exercise
Finding the Gateway

As with all things craft related, nighttime is great for doing workings, and this exercise is in particularly more engaging if done in the evening. Start with the alignment exercise and the earth and stellar darkness meditation. Once you feel fairly settled, rub your hands together and breathe into them a few times before encircling the candle with your hands. Breathe a breath of power into the candle and set an intention with the candle that it will open the book on your soul flight/hedge walking experience. It's encouraged that you write something on your own, but you could say something like the following:

> *By my breath and on this night*
> *I charge this candle for my rite*
> *Flame to wick I call to thee*
> *Spirits, open the gate for me*

Now, in the pitch black of your room, spark a match and light the wick. Feel its resonance through your space and how it creates a bubble of magickal energy around you. Spirits will draw near when you are intentional with your workings, but if you've done the work of warding your home, they should not be able to come any closer than you've allowed for. Odd things begin happening at times like these: you may notice the wind suddenly pick up or hear the call of a bird or wings flapping. These and more are good indicators that you're beginning to thin the veil between the worlds.

Focus as much of your attention as you can on the flame. Watch it dance and see how unseen and unfelt factors influence its movement. As you stay focused, try pouring your attention into the candle. Notice the space around and just above the wick where there is no flame and see how much it resembles a small gateway. Try peering through that gateway, focusing your attention on and through, and close your eyes. See the afterimage burned in your retinas. The light from the candle itself may begin to seep through your eyelids. Attempt to align the afterimage of the candlelight gateway with the light coming through. Open and close your eyes again to align the images and overlap them as precisely as possible. When you think you've succeeded, take a breath and exhale, blowing toward the flame. The light on your closed lids will dim—in that exact moment, look through the doorway. What do you see?

Do you see a figure or figures, landmarks, objects, colors, or landscapes? This is the first step on the hidden path and through the moonlit hedge. Your magick from this point forward will begin to awaken and become invigorated. What you see in that doorway is yours—it belongs to you and is part of you now and in has always been, in a way.

Now return yourself to normal consciousness, being careful to check in with yourself and ground any energies that you don't need. Take a moment to journal about your experience and dig deeply using the tools you've gathered so far. If you saw a figure, what or who did they look like? Was it an ancestor, a god/dess or some other entity? What impressions did you have of them? How did they make you feel? It's not always easy crossing thresholds, so don't be discouraged if it wasn't all sunshine and rainbows.

This exercise can show you where certain pain points still exist. If what stood on the other side scared or intimidated you, really try to uncover what it could mean. Is there a sensation that arises anywhere in your body? Could pain in your left hand, for example, indicate an imbalance somewhere that needs to be corrected? Work through as many possibilities as you can think of and if you're still coming up blank, relate your experience to a close friend, especially if they're a witch or someone who is psychically sensitive.

Often a close confidant will be able to quickly point out traits that are harder to grasp when you're too busy being wrapped up in being you. The aware practitioner seeks feedback and doesn't let their fears of judgment prevent real growth.

What you may encounter in this first glimpse really has no limit; sometimes I only see light, which I've interpreted to be a hopeful sign for the future or a reflection of my current state. Shapes, spirits, fears, the dead, even weather and animals have all been part of my personal experience.

If you truly saw nothing except perhaps the afterimage of the candle, take some time to meditate on why that might be. Could you be limiting yourself in some way or fearful that you could see something? Are you fearful that you might not be a witch? That doubt can be a powerful one. There's a certain amount of skepticism and rational thought that helps keep us anchored, and then there's the kind that shuts doors. Assess where you're at on the spectrum of skeptical inquiry versus full disbelief and remember that the Moon card can lead you to your shadows very quickly. Seeing nothing might not be bad at all, but it could be the shortcut that takes you to the crux of your dilemmas ... very powerful magick, indeed.

The Hedge Awaits

Here you are, back in the garden. The night is long and full of hungry mouths, yours among them. This is a good time to reflect on what a witch is: priestess or pariah, monster or mercy, medicine or poison? Is there any difference, or are we all these things at once? And who is doing the judging?

Sometimes the craft and journeywork requires you to do things you wouldn't consider in the light of day. Riding boneless is no easy business.

What are your limits beyond this garden? Will you be a carnivore with bloody claws and teeth, taking down your prey? Will you drift through, no more present than a mist or a whisper? What will you lose so that you might gain? What sort of sacrifice is too far, even for a witch as yourself?

Love can be found, light in abundance, but don't let your cultural programming fool you into thinking there's a way out of this without pain, yours and others. Without loss. Without darkness and death. These are all part of the complete experience, and those who shy from it will always find themselves wondering why things never seem whole.

Ask yourself, and ponder deeply, again, journal on it: Why do you want to cross the threshold, and are you prepared for the responsibility that comes with it?

Step one was finding the gateway and discover that it's within you. To leave, to enter other realms, you've discovered that to find the gateway you must first go within. And where it takes you is everywhere. Sometimes people only go through the gate once. that's all they need. They find the answer to whatever question they had and never feel inclined to return. Others return as the need arises, when challenging work needs to be done, when mountains need to be moved and monsters slain. Still others go regularly, addicted to going—over there they become lost, adrift, possessed by the need for escape or the desire to be in a world they find suits them better. These people are lost seekers and have brought too many complexes through the gateway with them. They become gaunt and ghoulish with hollow eyes and empty stares. There's feywild and then there's just lost. As Robert Graves' "The White Goddess" relates: "There is a stone seat at the top of Cader Idris, 'the Chair of Idris', where, according to the local legend, whoever spends the night is found in the morning either dead, mad, or a poet."[29] Graves's veracity as a historian has rightly been called into question, but poetic truths are still truths if we understand going in. Cader Idris is a real mountain in Wales, but it's equally true that Cader Idris is anywhere you make it. Sitting on my patio with a cat on my lap is Cader Idris if all the elements are right.

---

29. Robert Graves, *The White Goddess: A Historical Grammar of Poetic Myth* (London: Faber and Faber, 1952), 91.

When you journey through that gate, will you return dead, mad, or a poet? These are some of the choices; there could be more if you know how to look and where. Do you have the courage to confront your personal Cader Idris, to make the journey and spend the night atop the mountain? What do you hope to find? Where do you hope you'll be when you return? Will you return at all?

11.

The Witches' Sabbat

The witches' sabbat is a centerpiece of European and early American witch lore. While accusations against people meeting in secret for monstrous purposes such as infanticide, cannibalism, and orgies date back at least as early as the first century, it wasn't until the 1300s that the concept of the witches' sabbat as a conspiracy began to take root.[30] By the late 1400s, numerous texts existed detailing and describing characteristics of witches building upon the kernel of the idea.[31]

One writing that came about which was used as part of the witch trials of the early modern era was the *Malleus Maleficarum*, also known as the Hammer of Witches, by a Catholic clergyman named Heinrich Kramer. The concepts from this book among others published at the time were used repeatedly as manuals for the off-label purpose of persecuting and eliminating enemies, settling scores, and stealing land from people. Very few viable cases of witchcraft were found using the methods described in the *Malleus*, which generally encouraged torture at the hands of a psychopathic inquisitor to force a confession of basically anything the inquisitor suggested. Afterward, the unlucky accused was usually murdered in front of a crowd of family, friends, and neighbors. As Gutenberg's perfection of movable type set off the first true information revolution in at least a millennium, it sparked

---

30. Kelden, *The Witches' Sabbath: An Exploration of History, Folklore & Modern Practice* (Woodbury, MN: Llewellyn Worldwide, 2022), 10–12.

31. Ibid., 27–30.

the spread of more affordable books and pamphlets; as a byproduct, it fanned the flames of the witch hysteria.

From Then to Now

It truly cannot be stated enough that what we call witchcraft today did not exist all those centuries ago. As it lives in the Western mind today, witchcraft has been cultivated over the last several centuries out of a history of demonology created by the Catholic church and then picked up in Protestant communities. Romanticism and popular culture have since added layer upon layer in the form of books, art, and then radio, movies, television, and the internet as time progressed. We are living in the imaginal ponderings of our witchcraft ancestors; Margaret Murray's *The Witch-Cult in Western Europe* has been thoroughly disproven.

There were certainly herbalists, cunning men and women, and some areas of Europe who were holdouts of old practices that dated from before Christianity came through and forcibly eliminated their competition. Nevertheless, there are and always were spirits of place and people who knew how to work with them. Magick and people who know or can learn how to use have always existed. However, it is unlikely to the extreme that they would have self-identified as witches because the entire framework and fabric of their reality was bathed in the Christian mindset. In a way, the dualism that Christianity so egregiously spreads to this day is part of every one of our lived experiences. Most people in the West at least are comfortable with the concepts of good and evil and have a general sense of what they mean, even if they don't believe in the concepts. This is what the inescapability of your culture mean—it's in your programming, and your brain is replicating it even when you try to deprogram yourself. In the fifteenth century, you wouldn't want to be called a witch because they were servants of the devil, but even if you were capable of seeing through the lie as total nonsense, you wouldn't call yourself a witch because witches ended up dead. Full stop.

As a witch myself and one who consorts with spirits, yes, I know there is a mythological spirit who might align with the identity of the devil but in the same way I know there are other spirits who act as guardians of thresholds such as Hermes, Hecate, or other liminal beings. The devil at that point was an emissary from the wild world and the wild world can be threatening. In the Christian mindset of the early modern era, the church was the power that kept the wild world at bay, the force that fought and mastered it.

Equating nature with the devil makes it evil or at least unpalatable, which is why many with a Western upbringing aren't terribly invested in preserving wild places. Wild lands have been relegated into the realm of the dangerous and deadly while simultaneously being branded with terms like "fallow," "unused," or "undeveloped." These terms manage to turn something that existed in a state without human intercession for hundreds or thousands of years and transformed land everywhere into a possession to be done with whatever the owner feels like. The natural state of a patch of land isn't undeveloped or even owned, though even the term "wild" implies the need for mastery. The natural state of land just is.

When the church rapidly spread across the globe and gobbled up land and encountered problematic people, they were "clearly" in league with the sovereign ruler of that land, the devil himself. The people were maligned and their assets seized. It's a profitable little venture.

To this day, the Catholic Church is one of the largest non-governmental landholders in the world.[32, 33]

There very well could be a surviving cult of witches from ages past, but they would have to have a will of absolute iron and the luck of the devil himself to have lasted so long without being exposed.

What Was the Sabbat?

Members of the church promoted a legend that witches gather to create pacts and have orgies and all sorts of fun stuff all in league with the devil, of course.[34] It reads like entertainment, and it likely was for many who possessed

---

32. Anthony Leiserowitz, YCC Team, "The Catholic Church's vast landholdings could help protect the climate," Yale Climate Connections, June, 24, 2021, https://yaleclimateconnections .org/2021/06/the-catholic-churchs-vast-landholdings-could-help-protect-the-climate/.

33. "Church properties represent substantial assets," Fitzgerald Institute for Real Estate, University of Notre Dame, https://realestate.nd.edu/research/church-properties/.

34. Kelden, *Witches' Sabbath*, 27–30.

the books and pamphlets. At some point the spirit of fairness somehow visited, and it was decided that in order to be found guilty of witchcraft, you or your coven sisters (sometimes brothers) would have to confess that you participated in the Sabbat. They would have to report that you had taken part in *malefica*, (magick aimed at harming though magick of any kind was generally in the no-no category), and that you signed your name in the devil's book, et cetera—bonus points for giving your coveners' names. People were tortured and confessions were made for things that clearly never happened.

I'm relating this information because it's important to know that when we enact the witches' sabbat, we're participating in a fiction that the church itself helped propagate. That fiction didn't get passed in an unbroken line over centuries, but it was likely dug up and resurrected during an age when people had become dissatisfied with the answers Christianity had to offer about the purpose and meaning of life. Most likely, this fiction was pulled out of the dusty library of some upper class, bored, and thoroughly tired-of-the-religion-of-the-day man, who then brought it to some friends and decided to make a club where they practiced occult rites to thumb their noses at the social order.

More important is that where the kernel of modern witchcraft was borne from shouldn't change how you experience it. It's real today. And though the witchcraft we practice is not the same thing that our ancestors practiced, we are still using the tools and are possibly engaged in the same spirit they engaged with. The historical seizing and reclaiming of the sabbat was an act of justice. To take the framework created to make innocent people appear ghoulish, immoral, and outside the boundaries of what was societally acceptable was an immense act of restorative justice, and it is one that has helped heal a rift between humanity and the spirit world. It is a great joy to join the sabbat because it is reclaiming humanity's place within the natural order instead of othering it.

This is also a great time to talk about unverified personal gnosis (UPG). The original author of the witches' sabbat had probably heard stories or myths passed along that survived from some pre-Christian time and then wrote something they thought was maybe true, or it was manufactured whole cloth as an outright lie. We'll likely never know but if it was the former, it's what we call an act of unverified personal gnosis. In other words, it was something that they came to understand through deep meditation, reflection, and possible contact with gods or spirits but was not confirmed via others' separate experiences. UPG is typically frowned on today but there are so many countless pieces of present-day witchcraft's traditions that a short thirty or forty years ago were just that.

When someone proposes an idea or their experience with gods and spirits, it's UPG. But the minute other people begin verifying that they also have had a similar experience maybe after testing the original person's claims, it kind of becomes canon at that point. In a funny way, it's similar to how a show like *Supernatural* had its own writers and showrunners with their own ideas about the series and what it was versus the fan culture that came in and started creating their own fiction based on the characters, to the point that eventually some of those pieces got picked up and incorporated into the actual show. In that way, all lived experience was UPG at some point.

When I say that it doesn't matter that the sabbat wasn't real, it's not because I believe history doesn't matter—it certainly does. Mythmaking and storytelling are some of the most fundamental things that humans do, so by using the framework and taking a journey to a mythopoetic place, we've actually given it life. I'm going to make a controversial statement that will likely raise some hackles: nearly all the gods humans have worked with throughout time would not exist if there weren't humans to have worked with them. We breathe life into them, and they become bigger than us, and they become real. Gods aren't archetypes but they're also not *not* archetypes. When we begin to escape dualism, previously contradictory things begin to take form simultaneously.

One other potential source for the witches' sabbat may have been the wild hunt, a piece of folklore that originated in the Norse myths and bounced around northern Europe, picking up different cultural pieces and swapping out gods and riders along the way. The core of the story is that Odin would raise up his warriors who had been slain in battle for a raucous week or so (the timing is a little slippery) where he would ride his eight-legged steed at the front of a column of assembled spirits with whom he would gather up more souls. The wild hunt usually occurred in early winter after harvest time, when the cold was beginning to settle in. If you were unlucky enough to be walking about after dark during the wild hunt, you may well end up dead and joining the hunt.

Much like the witches' sabbat, the wild hunt was a collection of souls meeting at night during dangerous times to take part in dangerous and potentially deadly deeds. It's the perfect story for an invading culture to seize on and twist around for its own purposes. By turning the head of the whole thing into something that Christians would fear—the devil—it doesn't take a great deal of imagination to see how it might be used to other a culture resistant to indoctrination and then slowly use it as a tool to prove to the other culture, town by town, that they've been on the wrong team and now have an opportunity to join the right team.

The stories we tell create and destroy empires, breathe life into the dead and make the imaginal real. If you need a great example, look at the stories our media tell us each day and what we accept and patently reject based on our personal belief systems. In precisely this way, the stories Catholic leaders and authors in the 1400s created became a centerpiece of modern witchcraft, forming the experience and reverence for countless practitioners today. Someone picked this up and acted it out in body and in spirit; they breathed life into a story that was originally used for abhorrent purposes. They flipped the script in repudiation of what had been done. They essentially took a story and made a living temple out of it in the spirit realm that real spirits and gods visit... and where we can visit too. There's so much more to this existence than simple matter (in no small part because matter has animacy as well).

We're venturing down Alice's rabbit hole the closer we get to the heart of this but that's the beauty: the resonance of tens of thousands of people continuously visiting and joining in the witches sabbat have created a vibrant living thing with its own rules and behaviors.

Is the witches' sabbat manufactured or an amalgam? Does it matter? As a witch who has definitely never been a Christian, there is a small satisfaction in thinking that if it had originated as the wild hunt, taking the story back and at least symbolically trying to return it to its roots might be happening.

Crossing the Hedge to the Witches' Sabbat

Now that I've touched lightly on some of the history and theory behind the witches' sabbat, a great question comes up. Why should/would anyone want to venture there in the first place? The witches' sabbat can be viewed through many lenses, but maybe the most important is as both a cultural touchstone and a place of healing. There are many, many witches who don't include this or similar practices of venturing to the witches' sabbat in their experience of the craft, but many do. For those who use it and make it an important part of their practice, it affords them the possibility to discover new things, uncover hidden information, take on healing journeys, and commune with spirits new and familiar. It can also be viewed as a place where initiations happen, as hinted at earlier.

There are many stripes of initiation; this is one among them. There are bigger and small ones, those that are massively transformative and those with initiations in recognition of work already achieved. The best definition I can provide is that initiation is an event, spiritual or material, that alters or recognizes what has already changed within a person. The passing of a loved one, a graduation from school, and the reception of an award for hard work can all be initiations; after having gone through them, one is initiated, in a sense, into a group of people who have also had that experience. Most importantly, the initiated is marked by the experience in such a way that it changes them as a person.

In witchcraft as it's practiced in modern times—and specifically in the Wiccan community—initiations are very important recognitions of the work one has done and confers a new standing within that community and beyond. If you're a solitary practitioner, initiation can be an important sign of the progress and growth you've made in your craft, as you alone know the work you've put in and where you are on your path (regardless of the number of social media followers you have).

Another important consideration related to initiation is asking yourself: Am I ready? Doing the following working definitely marks a transition point for many people, the end of a chapter and the beginning of a new one. Consider consulting astrology or divinatory methods, such as tarot or runes, to gain some clarity on your situation. And most importantly, check in with yourself. Is your ego still driving the car when you consider the question? When you look back at the work you've done in this book, do you feel satisfied with what you've accomplished, or are there any exercises you'd like to revisit?

In a goal-oriented and competitive culture, it can be hard to step aside, take a breath, and honestly assess where we are. Maybe it's the Taurus in me, but I'm probably on the flip side, taking too long, dragging decisions out, and not wanting to move until all possible outcomes have been *thoroughly* explored. I'd say that it drives my partner nuts but she's a Taurus too!

Initiations

There's no two ways about it: when you endeavor to cross the threshold of spirit and enter that gateway, you're engaging in an initiatory rite. Once upon a time, we lived in a world that valued structured initiation. There were rites that occurred after birth (birth itself is a massive initiation for the birthing and the birthed), there were (and in some cultures still are) naming ceremonies, baptisms, and the like. The entry into adulthood was another that in our culture and age has by large part gone absent. For the most part, the ritual passages that still exist if you happen to be of a faith that still observes them are just formality: some words are said, some water splashed, some incense blown on you, maybe you come out of it with a little less skin. The community that surrounded these actions, made them important, and were united in their enduring an initiatory event are all pretty well gone.

More than any of those previously mentioned, the entry into adulthood is perhaps the most problematic. When I was a child, most adults still acted like children. When I became an adult, I did as well because that was the total of what our culture was capable of bestowing. This society has become a society of children, children who are frightened and petty, adrift and directionless. Truly, becoming a witch means stepping away from that; it comes with responsibility, the most important of which is asking ourselves if we are prepared to commit our lives to this work of spiritual development and rigorous discipline. It's a commitment to ourselves that will require honesty and reflection, a willingness to turn otherness into an ally, to work with and through our foibles and demons.

As someone who has crossed through that doorway several times and for several reasons, I want to tell you that this is a big choice to make. While you aged into being an adult without instruction, this is one moment in which you have free will but you will absolutely be welcomed into a community that is eager to provide instruction.

So now that I feel like the infamous Lestat character from Anne Rice's *Vampire Chronicles* series, I'm "going to give you the choice I never had." Beloved and hokey bloodsuckers aside, it's time to jump into your own Tom Cruise/Brad Pitt initiation moment as we journey to the witches' sabbat.

When you decide you're ready and know that you would like to join a community of spirit, move ahead with the following exercise.

In preparation, spend some time journaling about what you would like to experience of the craft and what skills you have that you'll be able to offer. Make sure that you've partnered with spirits of place or ancestors as they will help lend you support (Meeting your spirit guides chapter) and write them down. Finally, journal about something that you'd be comfortable with leaving behind, a habit, a trait, how you react in certain situations. Just make sure it's something that you are 100% ready to release.

There will be two parts to the guided journey. You only need to do the first part, the second part is completely optional and will be noted as such in the text. If you want to have a deeper experience of this work, consider creating an audio version of the text and playing it while you make the journey to guide you.

Exercise
Joining the Sabbat

As always, get comfortable, light some incense if you like, and dim the lights. Light your main candle and sit at your altar space. Align yourself and do earth and stellar darkness meditation.

Begin chanting the names of the spirits with which you're aligned, listing one at a time until you feel them enter the space. When they've all appeared, begin spiraling their names in succession to weave a circle around you and create sacred space for your work.

As you did in the previous chapter, meditate on the candle flame: watch its flicker and dance in the subtle shifts of air around you. Take note if it's active or still and then let it all fade away until it's just you in the black void of the universe, floating in front of this single flame, the flame of existence that represents all the stars that ever were, that represents all life that ever has been or will be. Watch as the flame drinks in the darkness and pulls everything toward it. Notice the small doorway at the bottom of the flame. Feel all the energy consumed by the flame moving through that gateway to what awaits on the other side. From the other side, a dim light shines through and grows steadily in intensity. You know it's the light of the entire universe, and it becomes almost too bright for your eyes but then you recognize it as the starlit path, a familiar path that you've walked before but this time, it leads straight through the gate.

If you allow the energies to pull you through—if you choose to take the starlit path to the witches' sabbat—you feel squeezed as you pass through. It's clear that you'll have to leave something behind to make it through. Now is the time to let go of what you've been clinging to, the thing you journaled about before the start of this journey. Sacrifice is mandatory, so what will you lose in order to move forward?

Feel yourself release it. In being unburdened, you feel buoyant enough to ascend through the gateway. As you float through, a brilliant light and awesome sound erupts around you, and you find yourself in absolute darkness. Your awareness returns to your body and you realize that you're standing. Feel the weight of your body settle and anchor you. As your eyes adjust to the very dim light, you realize you feel cold and are in a forest illuminated only by distant stars that look down at you through the tops of trees. A light wind picks up and seems to gently push you in a direction. As best you can tell, the ground is covered in leaves. Though there is no trail, the ground is fairly level and easy to walk along. Distantly, you hear the sound of drums carried across the hills and through the forest. You can vaguely tell which direction they're coming from and begin to head that way, knowing that the answers you seek are that way.

The closer you get, you notice the sounds of others, other feet shuffling through the fallen foliage. Suddenly, the tree line breaks in front of you and you see that you're perched atop a bluff looking down. Others like you are stepping from out of the woods, shining eyes alight with the flames from a bonfire in the middle of the clearing. Around the fire are dozens and dozens, maybe a hundred or more forms, and still more continue to join. There are humans, not quite humans, monstrous creatures, fey, the spirits of the dead, animals, and awesome energies that defy description, chanting, playing drums and musical instruments, singing and dancing. Some faces you recognize. Many of the beings are partially clothed, and some are engaged in various sex acts. It's an orgy of feasting and celebrating. This is the witches' sabbat, the eternal dance and celebration of the wild world.

You realize that there's nowhere to go back to now, even if you wanted to. The only way is forward. As you step from the forest into the clearing, the music stops and all eyes fall to you.

The only noise now is the sound of your footfalls and the crackling of the bonfire in the center of the clearing.

"Will you join us, child?" you hear the voice and then see a face; it may be familiar to you or wholly new.

You know you have freedom in this decision. If you decide no, you're awakened from your trance in the room where you began this working; your journey is done for now, but you may choose to return when you feel ready.

If you say yes, the figure steps forward and unties a small pouch from its belt and places it in your hand. You loosen the strings of the pouch and it falls open to reveal a mushroom. The figure nods its head and you know that it wants you to consume the mushroom.

If you take a bite, the crowd roars around you, guttural sounds, screams of joy and terror and ecstasy, and with the stomping of feet and beating of drums, the celebration renews with even greater vigor than before.

As you chew the mushroom, you feel a warmth spread through your body like rivulets of water running down to each of your extremities. The stars above begin to swirl and dance— but are they really stars or the lights of a hundred thousand fireflies?

You feel compelled to join the dance, to join the merrymaking and festivities. As you do, you lose yourself to the powers of this world. Where before you saw only chaos and perhaps madness in the crowd's movements and sounds, you now hear beautiful music and glorious singing. You feel elated at how connected and at one you are with everyone here. Dancing and singing, faster and faster, each face becomes a reflection of your own, each movement seen as through a mirror. In this place you are the universe, dancing with itself, singing with itself, in complete recognition of itself.

Relish in the power of this moment for as long as you care to. When you are finished, the figure comes once again to you. The crowd once again grows quiet.

"Today, which is every day, which is beyond time and all of time, I introduce …" and they say your name—not your name that you're used to but something new but very old. When you hear it, it's like a bell is rung in your mind. They say the name three times and the crowd applauds. Several figures rush forward to greet you by this name.

This is your hidden name, the name that only those who wear and dispose of veils, who crash through barriers and balance on the edge of a knife, may know. Cherish it as you would a child, keep it safe from those who would use it against you—it's a key that grants you passage forever onwards through many gates.

The figure says to you "Now, child, it's time to go" before kissing your cheek and presenting you to the crowd again to one last round of applause.

"You may return as you feel the need, but for now, rest is required," they say as they lead you to a huge tree just on the edge of the clearing. The tree's roots are exposed, as if the soil wore away ages ago, exposing an intricate weaving. As you grow closer, you see what appears to be an entry into the base, beneath the tree where the roots have parted in the shape of a gateway.

"Our roots feed one another, our flesh feeds the earth, our souls are familiar, always," the figure says and turns back to the sabbat.

As you pass through the roots beneath the tree, you step back into your body in the here and now.

Welcome to the great mysteries of the craft! As you ease back into your own consciousness, make sure to jot down a few of your memories of the biggest things you experienced. Most importantly, remember the name you were given and keep it safe! Now is also a good time to do the grounding exercise. If you feel as though you've brought any energies back with you, focus on them during the grounding. If truly necessary, do the exercise to cut energetic cords.

If this is your first time experiencing an initiatory experience in the witch-craft context, spend time ruminating on what it means for you. This expe-rience was very personal but really, they all are. It's important to note the difference from this initiatory experience and a true initiation bestowed by another practicing member of the craft. Recall that an initiation in a Wic-can (and some other witchcraft) tradition is very different and usually involve weaving yourself into the current of power unique to them.

This experience is slightly different because you're making a commitment to yourself and the beings and spirits who embody the craft that you are now and ever shall be a walker of hedges and a witch. There are variations on what that even means (Terry Pratchett famously said the real word for a group of witches is "an argument") but as far as I'm concerned, if you've come this far you've earned it.[35]

Next Steps

From here, your next steps are up to you. You came in with free will and you leave with it. If you choose to never do another witchcraft thing in your life, it's all the same to me. There are plenty of schools, traditions, classes, and more that you can explore in addition to countless books to read and pod-casts to listen to. One thing that I frequently remind myself is that reading fiction can be just as much an enhancement of your craft as reading books on the practice of the craft. Poetry too, maybe even more so.

Keep the magick alive by committing to a daily practice that can scale up or down depending on your available time. My days include at a minimum a prayer to the Star Goddess and some variation on many of the exercises included in this book. On many days, I try to do much more. If you can't commit to less than five minutes a day to your craft, that's fine but keep it in mind and maybe set it as a goal for the future.

---

35. Terry Pratchett, *Wintersmith* (New York: HarperTempest, 2006), 94.

Finally, keep the connection alive with any spirits you met on this journey, especially those with whom you found kinship. Ask what they want in return for what they offer, and if their request seems safe and reasonable, do it. Sometimes they just want a companion for a little while on this mysterious journey we're all on together.

Nothing in this world is mundane, so don't let people convince you otherwise. Every atom in every insect, person, and tree is magickal, and the whole world responds to your presence. Let's take these tools and reawaken humanity from its slumber. The forces of narcissism, avarice, selfishness, and hate cannot be the last message of humanity. Witches are possessed with the voice of the wild world. Let that voice be heard.

Conclusion:
All Paths Under the Moonlight

It's been said that witchcraft is the lonely road that witches travel together. Each witch represents a thread of the whole—in a grand metaphysical sense, we are all just atoms, each of us part of the one witch who presides over creation and shifts the tides of being with her magick, part of the one fabric that we contribute to for a time and for all time.

Hopefully this book has outlined a path for you. It is one I have personally pursued and crafted for myself over the course of a decade or more. Along the way, I was inspired by some great teachers who you can see in the acknowledgements. No witch lives in a void; though they may travel the path alone, every one of us influences and is influenced in return by ideas old and new, different approaches, and wonderful, meaningful magick.

As you may be able to tell, my influences are varied: from druidry, witchcraft, and Buddhism to the Stoic philosophers and a pernicious thread of the Sacred Fool from whom I have learned through humor and daring that fun is its own sacred tool. Equally, my teachers have been the plants that I talk to every day, the fungi and lichen, the animals and slowly flowing waters of the Everglades. The rapidly moving waters of my home river, the Mississippi. The winds and breezes, the whispering huldufolk, fae, wights, land spirits, my ancestors who I try to do right by. The various gods and goddesses, and the great Star Goddess from whom we all emerge and to whom we all return.

Through the journeys, healings, and meditations you've read here, I hope a path has emerged for you and you are inspired to take from these teachings what you can to improve the world with your craft.

Through journeys of healing, through pathways of mending your schisms, by doing this work, you are freeing yourself to approach the great work of the craft with more openness, sincerity, and energy.

Fostering a world view of relationality in which you fall in love with each moment and each being you encounter (even though it opens you to some risks) is a momentous step forward. This world needs witches who are working on healing and expanding empathy for others. We don't need more light workers; we need more compassion workers who are listeners, those who take their magick seriously and who aren't preoccupied with the overculture's binary moralism that fits a witch as well as socks on a snake. We need those listen to the voices of the pine warblers and hawkmoths and sundew and stinkhorn, who see these beings as members of our greater family and community here on earth.

This is the end of time, if we dare to make it, and the end of an epoch whether we want it or not. The overculture, mediocre apologists, and extraction-obsessed tech industry are feeding us all a narrative that this is an era of destruction and powerlessness. We are told that we are incapable of making change so we may as well go with what we're told and agree to their version of reality. You don't have to consent to that. Reality is a group project, always; I can tell you that mine is quite different—how about yours?

Take it from someone who thought they were a lifelong pessimist until they realized that they were just agreeing to someone else's story: things can be different. The more of us who believe it, the more real it becomes.

We're not going to solve climate change, right? It's insurmountable at this point and will leave the earth a leveled hellscape, uninhabitable for our species and the countless species we take down with us. Right? It's been said, though not loudly and not in the most rigidly managed channels, that the challenges we face with climate change will likely be less impactful than the actual struggle our species went through for 99 percent of its time on earth.

Our life spans may shorten, but they won't be shorter than the drastic forty years that characterized most of humanity's existence. Even hearing something like this is so out of the ordinary that it has the power to shake us from the fugue of what the current twenty-first century's current narrative.

True hope propels action, is expansive and inclusive, and is buffeted and buoyed by inquiry, not beleaguered by it. The magick of hope comes from deepening relationships with others—human and non-human beings—alike. It is always bold to believe that things can be different, but that change must first happen internally and that the view of an enchanted world must be present. Crass materialism coupled with an ideology that views the human soul(s) as momentarily housed in flesh only to return to some greater, other world has been a disaster. The lie that we're not from here is so endlessly perpetuated that it's become insinuated into lifeways that never were compatible with it.

It's time to think differently and to act differently. We all have skin in this game because even if we spend some time out of body or extra-dimensionally, we'll be back in one form or fashion. Hopefully if you return as a dung beetle or a loblolly pine, you'll have the benefit of encountering other beings attuned to consulting with you about our mutual paths forward. I am not being cheeky about this—it's what I sincerely hope.

What do mountains want? What do forests or swamps want? Do they have needs like we do? How would we know? The first and best thing to do is to start talking to them. Start experiencing them. One of the biggest health problems that humans experience right now that arguably supersedes many of our other conditions, is a disconnection from the natural world. Because we've stopped thinking about ourselves as part of it, our consciousness and ability to communicate with it have become divorced from it. Anxiety, depression, diabetes, high blood pressure, all the ills of modern society flow from that one soul wound. How much of your witchcraft is done in nature? I have altars (plural) in my home, but most of the magick I do is done outside, more often than not with sweat rolling down my back and bugs biting me. And it's there that some of the most powerful working occurs.

A Witch of the Moonlit Hedge

What does it mean to be a witch of the moonlit hedge, and what does a path forward look like? In some ways, it's what we've always dreamed it to be. She settles on the edges of the world, even if that's in the middle of a large city. She winds back and forth over the hedgerows and meets new beings, makes pacts and friendships along the way that can change humanity. She partners with the ancient presences that dot the earth, those still living, meeting them at the crossroads.

From sea to mountain to prairie and desert, we spread our mycelial threads of connection. We send energy and connection and receive it in return. We become wild things that walk with poise and purpose. We grow and are nourished by our partnerships with the living land and reverberate change where we are to shift the story of humanity because we are the storytellers and the thread of the story is ours to control now.

It's not a single path we walk but one among many we are growing organically. As we work with the shifting rhythms of the changing planet, it will in turn respond to our presence.

This is my prayer to the Great Goddess of All, please join me on this path.

Appendix:
Additional Exercises

Included here are some additional exercises that didn't make their way into the original text but are important to include. They're next-step work such as blessings, banishings, and cleansings. I've included my personal candle blessing and banishing exercises that make up a good chunk of my own spellwork.

Blessing or Consecrating

Blessing or consecrating is an ancient practice that you can do with just about anything or anyone around you. Bless your shoes, bless your sofa, bless your microwave, and your wand. Bless everything! Reasons for doing so vary but generally, the goal is to make or re-make something holy. There's a lot of arguments you can get into here, especially as an animist: since everything is enspirited, isn't all of it already holy? Let's think of a blessing or consecration as a type of cleansing that might also add a small boon or bit of extra energy to whatever our subject is.

The simplest way to bless something is to align yourself and call upon the primary source to which you attune your energies—a god or goddess, the blessed spirit of She-Ra, nature, whatever, so long as you have a sincere and deep connection. And no, this doesn't preclude atheists; the universe is a perfectly suitable and non-theistic source to rely on.

Connect with that source and ask that the subject of your blessing be given every advantage, that all obstacles and distractions are removed from it, and that it acts as a living embodiment of that source. If using an anointing

oil or spray, use that on the subject. Do little workings like this whenever you begin working with a new tool, on items (such as herbs, stones, leaves, string, dirt, etc.) that will be used in casting a spell, or before imbuing an item with whatever energies you're after.

Exercise
Preparing the Candle

Candle blessings are great workings that can continue spreading their good vibes for as long as your candle is lit and beyond, as the energy of the blessing will still fill your house long after.

There are many good books on candle dressing, but the basics are simple and limited only by your creativity. Using a candle that aligns colorwise with your intent is a good place to start. White is a great, all-purpose color, perfect for a blessing; you could also use blue to bring a calm and peaceful feeling, yellow to help brighten the mood in your home, and so on. There are a million websites, Pinterest boards, TikToks, et cetera that feature color correspondences, so it's easy to dial in exactly what kind of energy you need. Because we're just doing a general blessing, we'll stick to the white candle.

Use runes or other symbols or write a charm on the outside of your candle using a pin, needle, or an awl. You can draw or scratch any symbol that stands for health, happiness, protection, etc. to you. Another option are sigils (books on crafting them are helpful). I tend to use runes, bindrunes (amalgams of multiple runes), or personal sigils. Using oils, dress the candle by rubbing it all around the surface of the candle. Some witches like to anoint the candles in a certain direction (clockwise or anti-clockwise) to bring in or cast something away. You can use the Florida Water from earlier in the book or you can use essential oils like myrrh or frankincense (can't beat the classics) or citrus and citrus-adjacent scents for a more joyful energy. Other popular oils include sweet orange, neroli, grapefruit, and bergamot.

The last step to candle dressing comes with a caveat: fire hazard ahead. While oils can potentially increase fire hazards, dressing a candle in herbs *absolutely* increases the risk of fire hazards. It's usually best to dress with herbs when using spell or chime candles. For a blessing candle that you intend to leave burning for an extended period, the best practice is not to use it at all, though it can be a lovely part of the practice and helps add even more oomph. Any herbs you plan on using should be dried and ground in a mortar and pestle or using the modern magician's holy coffee grinder. People wrinkle their noses at coffee grinders until they're tasked with grinding up bay leaves, which are top of the blessing list. After twenty minutes of attempting to mortar and pestle up bay leaves, you'll likely be ready to throw a boot through the window; you've been warned.

If you want to get really high-falutin with your magick, you can also include other correspondences such as planetary hours and days, lunar phases, and astrological timing, all depending on how much time you have ahead of the need you're addressing with your candles. For a simple blessing candle, you could create and dress your candles on a Sunday during the hour of the sun or the hour of Venus to capture some loving, joyful energy.

We won't get too much into planetary hours here; there are many books and even apps that do the work of calculating the daylight and nighttime hours for you, in addition to calculating the planetary days (both of which are different from standard sixty-minute, twenty-four-hour blocks of time).

Timing taken into consideration or no, you can now bless your candle. It's up to you whether you bless it in a circle or not; many witches say that magick can only be done in a circle. I beg to differ—people in need have always used magick when in need. If you have time and space, a circle offers many benefits, including protection and a consecrated space allowing you to function as a true creator. That said, magick done outside a circle is just as valid.

Exercise
Candle Blessing

Begin by aligning and then move on to the earth and stellar darkness meditation. Call to your favorite deity/non-deity flavor and ask for their (or its) blessing in your work. Begin breathing. We're going to awaken our candle by breathing life into it, breathing up from the earth. Through your feet, you will pull a small amount of energy up as you inhale and breathe it out into the candle. See the earth energy fill the candle until it is golden and radiant in your psychic vision. Once the candle is filled with this powerful energy, you may stop and speak to the candle:

> *I awaken this candle and fill it with the energies*
> *of the earth. I awaken this candle that it may serve as a tool of*
> *cleansing and blessing. I awaken this candle to radiate blessings*
> *throughout time and space, cleansing and blessing all space*
> *and all beings who have need of its energy.*

Whatever you used—herbs, oils, planetary hours, et cetera—you can mention in addition to what each of those items bring. For example:

> *I draw upon the blessings of the sun on this Sunday and utilize and*
> *amplify its powers during the hour of the sun to bring support*
> *and blessings to this working. I draw upon the plant spirit of bay to*
> *add its blessing and protecting energy. I call upon the invigorating and*
> *joyful energy of neroli to be present in my working. (etc, etc)*

If you like, you can also name a deity or other powerful spirit to lend their influence. There's really no limit when doing a working; just make sure you're working with the right spirits and have an established relationship with any that you ask.

Your candle should now feel vibrant and alive with energy. When you put your hands near it, you should get a sensation akin to how two similarly charged magnets repel each other— subtle but noticeable.

You can end the work with a simple statement of gratitude to all the spirits you called upon during your working and make a small offering of some sort, e.g., some incense, food, or a libation. Just remember that after you offer it, it belongs to them. Don't get side-tracked and drink the gods' apple juice.

When you want to cleanse a space, light up your candle and feel the good vibes.

Banishing

Some folks find the work of banishing a little distasteful. It's difficult to discern why but if I had to guess, there's an element of "dark" working that goes along with it that a lot of people who work in dualistic modalities find unsettling. The witchcraft I practice runs the spectrum from black to white and back again with a happy little rainbow in the middle. One of the important parts of being a witch is creating your own set of ethical rules and boundaries, what you will and will not do. That said, there's value in exploring rather than rejecting a working you've decided on first (or second, or third) inspection to be bad. Consider reasons why you're uncomfortable and ask yourself where those reasons originate from. There are countless things I won't do with my magick, and then there are the if/thens. If *this* were to happen, then I would be comfortable doing *that*. You can get into some tricky thought experiments, but it's a good time to have them when you're not in a quandary.

Some workings stay with a person indefinitely until the condition is lifted, so consider what it might mean for that person to carry a hex and if that's something you want to have on your conscience. The person doing the working and the target are linked with each other afterward; unless you know how to properly cleanse and uncross yourself, you might carry an echo of the energy you put out in the world. This is all food for thought; some of it may never apply to you. Some of the most powerful magicians and witches are those who others know carry real power, and sometimes that's all the deterrent that's needed.

For this introduction to banishing, we'll keep it fairly neutral so you don't have to worry if you're crossing ethical boundaries before you've established what they are.

A good practice that goes hand in wand with blessing your house is getting rid of the critters you find hanging out that you don't want. Just like you wouldn't want rats or roaches taking up residence in your home, you also don't want spiritual pests hanging around either. In *The Witch's Shield*, Christopher Penczak talks about something one of his friends termed "little nasties," a name that stuck with me, and I continue to use.[36] Little nasties are sort of like the mosquitos of the spirit world. The idea goes that when we as witches come in contact with our spiritual power, we "light up" in the spirit world and cast a radiance that attracts all sorts of little pests. These little nasties siphon off bits of your magickal power or mana, your life force, providing another reason why having good shields is important to your practice.

Of all places, your home should be free of these things for obvious reasons. If there were a cloud of mosquitos just outside your door, you wouldn't slide it open and invite them to feast on you, right? (Reminder: I live in Florida, land of sliding glass doors). In the same way, you want to have shields or wards that prevent them from entering, and you want to have an effective tool for getting rid of the ones that have snuck in. A psychic fly swatter. We won't be smushing any of these nuisances, though if you've got a soft spot for parasites for some reason, we'll just be ushering them out.

Exercise
Preparing the Banishing Candle

There are a couple ways you can go about banishing; since candles were mentioned earlier, we'll start there. Get a candle, preferably black and definitely small. Look for spell candles online, at your metaphysical retailer, or just use a birthday candle. Getting fancy

---

36. Christopher Penczak, *The Witch's Shield* (Woodbury, MN: Llewellyn Publications, 2008), 19. Quoting Donald Michael Kraig's *Modern Magick* (St. Paul, MN: Llewellyn Publications, 2001), 76.

is fun and helps juice up a spell more easily by getting you more into it, but sometimes you have to work with what you've got. Also grab a needle, it can be a sewing needle, bobby pin, safety pin, you get the idea. Last, grab a mason jar with a lid. If you want to get real fancy, get a piece of magnetized hematite to set next to the jar.

On the candle you can etch runes or use shapes that have resonance for you. If etching isn't for you, you can also anoint the candle with an oil such as frankincense or myrrh, anything with a high potency kick that will bring the little buggers quick. We're going to use this candle to attract, capture, and remove unwanted entities from our house. Think of it like the ghost trap in Ghostbusters.

After you've fixed the candle, carefully melt the end of it so that you can stick it to the bottom of the jar. It should harden quickly. As soon as it has, fill the jar with water about halfway up the candle. If the candle loosens, start over and really get it stuck to the bottom.

Exercise
Candle Banishing

Before you light your candle, take a moment to align yourself and bless all the parts of it if you haven't already. If you work with any spirits, you can ask for their help as well. For this working, I would ask the energy of something that you've worked with before that has a trap setting quality to it, e.g., the pitcher plant, Venus fly trap, or trapdoor spider. Now call upon the Goddess, universe, most powerful She-Ra, etc., and say:

I empower this candle to attract unwanted entities from the bounds of my property. I empower this jar to act as a trap that holds the entities within it until I can remove them from my property. I shield myself from them and hold myself immune from their influence. So mote it be.

Now light the candle and let the trap do its thing. When the candle begins to sizzle, you'll know that the trap is almost set. When the water extinguishes it, put the lid on and remove it from your property. What you do from there is up to you. I'd pour the water out on the earth and toss the candle in a dumpster and recycle or reuse the jar later (just clean and cleanse it). When you do get rid of it, remember: shield, shield, shield! You don't want any little nasties catching a free ride with you right back into your house.

Exercise
Forcing Out with the Psychic Bubble

This exercise is another method for banishing. The idea is simpler to grasp but the amount of energy required of the practitioner is greater.

Align yourself and then perform the shield exercise. Imagine your shield as a flexible entity rather than a rigid shield, more like a bubble and less like a quartz shell. Set the parameters for the shield:

> *I empower this shield to force out all unwanted entities in my household and from my property. I call upon the power of (God/dess, universe, etc) to aid me in my request and banish these unwanted entities, scattering them like leaves before a powerful wind. So mote it be.*

Now visualize your shield growing larger and larger around you. With each inhale, the shield grows more until it has surpassed the walls of the room you're in, the walls of your house, and finally out to the edges of the property.

Exercise
Creating a Ward

Now that you have this etheric bubble around your home, it's a good idea to set it as a ward. Wards are an extension of a shield that encompasses a larger area, including your property or even your vehicle.

To use the expanded bubble shield as a ward, say:

I ward this home from all people, spirits, or other entities who come in bad faith. I ward this home from all who would come to harm, knowingly or not. I protect this home and set this ward as a barrier and create a refuge for any who come with good intent. So mote it be.

Setting a ward is usually something often done separately, mostly because it'll be renewed them rather than remade from scratch. When renewing wards, it's good practice to focus them on a symbol or sigil—a pentacle is perfect. Draw one on your door or some other entryway to the home and imagine the ward originating there and radiating out to the edges of your property.

Warding is just as effective with apartments—you can set wards that reach to the edges of your own apartment. For more advanced work, you could set multiple wards, one for your personal property and another much more general one that encompasses your building.

Cleansing

One day, I went to a grocery store in my in-law's neighborhood to pick up some things. We were housesitting for them, so it wasn't a store that I normally visit. When I passed through the doors, I immediately felt a thick, gross, energy. It really felt like someone just socked me in the gut. In my mind's eye I saw flashes of people crying, blood spatter on the produce, and I heard a lot of loud noise. I felt physically ill and couldn't shake it. The workers who were stocking shelves looked normal to my regular vision but looked dead-eyed and haunted in my psychic senses. Normally I'm pretty well shielded when I go out in public; I find people's energy to be too contagious and overwhelming, so that this much was breaking through really was remarkable. There was a sense of profound loss that was haunting the store, and I knew that someone or multiple people had lost their lives there and it had happened recently enough that the environment itself was still in a trauma state.

Discernment is an important skill to develop as you work in the craft. There are people and places who do not want our help, and we have to be okay with that. It would be rude at a minimum and potentially a violation to do a love spell for someone without their knowledge or consent. Even to send people healing and supportive energy when they're ill without them knowing and agreeing to it can be construed as crossing a line if they're not someone who would appreciate that kind of thing (I'm looking at you, evangelical relatives). It's not for us to decide what's best for anyone, but we can offer to help. If the person or entity declines, then we move on.

Back in the grocery store, I slowed down and spent time closely examining some produce. While I was doing that, I started to connect with and converse with the spirit of the land on which this grocery store sat. It was overcome with a sense of what I would identify as grief and shock, and it had the resonance of this event still ringing through it. I didn't think I could eliminate it entirely, but I thought I might be able to help filter the energy and make it less dense by doing a blessing. I got the sense that it was eager for my help when I offered it, so I began my work. I'm not eager to draw attention to myself or get managers involved, so I definitely do not go full woo in this scenario. No robes or theatrical voices; no chanting and cleansing incense. Just street clothes and a stone or two that I frequently keep in my pocket. But I did align myself, and do the tree meditation, very briefly. I then opened up my heart space and began pulling the energy into it with the intention that I was simply filtering out the bad elements and grounding them into the earth to be broken down. The rest of the energy I would just breathe out, allowing it to return from where it came. At no time did I use any of the energy myself; I simply walked slowly around, for all appearances just another thoughtful shopper working through his grocery list. Aisle by aisle, step by step, I blessed and cleansed the whole store. When it was done, there was a particular shine to the place that hadn't been there before. I connected with the land spirit once again and it seemed much more at ease.

Later, I found out that a particularly horrific shooting had occurred there (they're all horrific), but this one shocked me. I was glad to have had the opportunity to address some of the negativity and help heal the wound that had been festering there for a little while.

The style of cleansing I did was a little more advanced and might be considered risky if you don't know what you're doing. The last thing you want is for some of that energy to attach itself to you. But there are other ways one can cleanse, the easiest being to use consecrated oil or water and asperge (fancy word for sprinkling, sometimes done with a small branch from an herb such as rosemary or a small tree branch), or just do like I do and use a spray bottle.

Selected Bibliography

Abram, David. *The Spell of the Sensuous: Perception and Language in a More-Than-Human World*. New York: Vintage Books, 1997.

Allione, Tsultrim. *Feeding Your Demons: Ancient Wisdom for Resolving Inner Conflict*. New York: Little, Brown and Company, 2008.

Anderson, Cora. *Fifty Years in the Feri Tradition*. Portland, OR: Harpy Books, 1994.

———. *In Mari's Bower: A Biography of Victor H. Anderson*. Portland, OR: Harpy Books, 2010.

———. *Kitchen Witch*. Portland, OR: Harpy Books, 2008.

Anderson, Victor. *Etheric Anatomy: The Three Selves and Astral Travel*. Albany, CA: Acorn Guild Press, 2004.

———. *The Heart of the Initiate: Feri Lessons*. Portland, OR: Harpy Books, 2010.

Bookchin, Murray. *The Philosophy of Social Ecology: Essays on Dialectical Materialism*. Chico, CA: AK Press, 2022.

Coyle, T. Thorn. *Evolutionary Witchcraft*. New York: Tarcher/Penguin, 2005.

———. *Kissing the Limitless*. Newburyport, MA: Weiser Books, 2009.

Debord, Guy. *Comments on the Society of the Spectacle*. London: Verso Books, 1998.

Dominguez, Jr., Ivo. *Keys to Perception: A Practical Guide to Psychic Development*. Newburyport, MA: Weiser Books, 2017.

———. *The Four Elements of the Wise: Working with the Magickal Powers of Earth, Air, Water, Fire.* Newburyport, MA: Weiser Books, 2021.

Faerywolf, Storm. *Betwixt and Between: Exploring the Faery Tradition of Witchcraft.* Woodbury, MN: Llewellyn Worldwide, 2017.

Gagliano, Monica. *Thus Spoke the Plant: A Remarkable Journey of Groundbreaking Scientific Discoveries and Personal Encounters With Plants.* Berkeley, CA: North Atlantic Books, 2018.

Goodenough, Ursula. *The Sacred Depths of Nature.* New York: Oxford University Press, 1998.

Gray, Patience. *Honey from a Weed.* London: Prospect Books, 2009.

Grey, Peter. *Apocalyptic Witchcraft.* n.p.: Scarlet Imprint, 2013.

Grimassi, Raven. *Old World Witchcraft: Ancient Ways for Modern Days.* San Francisco: Weiser Books, 2011.

Haskell, David George. *The Songs of Trees: Stories from Nature's Great Connectors.* New York: Penguin, 2017.

Hooker, Eleanor. *The Shadow Owner's Companion.* Dublin, Ireland: Dedalus Press, 2012.

Howe, Katherine, ed. *The Penguin Book of Witches.* New York: Penguin Books, 2014.

Hughes, Ted. *The Birthday Letters.* New York: Farrar Straus Giroux, 1998.

Kahn, Langston. *Deep Liberation: Shamanic Teachings for Reclaiming Wholeness in a Culture of Trauma.* Berkeley, CA: North Atlantic Books, 2021.

Kelden. *The Witches' Sabbath.* Woodbury, MN: Llewellyn Worldwide, 2022.

Kirk, Robert. *The Secret Commonwealth of Elves, Fauns and Fairies.* New York: New York Review Books, 2007.

Leland, Charles Godfrey. *Aradia: Gospel of the Witches.* New York: Cosimo, 2007.

Oliver, Mary. *Dream Work.* New York: The Atlantic Monthly Press, 1986.

Penczak, Christopher. *The Inner Temple of Witchcraft.* Woodbury, MN: Llewellyn Worldwide, 2002.

Penczak, Christopher. *The Mighty Dead.* Salem, NH: Copper Cauldron, 2013.

———. *The Outer Temple of Witchcraft.* Woodbury, MN: Llewellyn Worldwide, 2004.

———. *The Temple of Shamanic Witchcraft*. Woodbury, MN: Llewellyn Worldwide, 2005.

Schama, Simon. *Landscape and Memory*. New York: Vintage Books, 1995.

Steindl-Rast, David. *Gratefulness, the Heart of Prayer: An Approach to Life in Fullness*. New York: Paulist Press, 1984.

Valiente, Doreen. *Where Witchcraft Lives*. n.p.: The Doreen Valiente Foundation, 2014.

Watts, Alan. *The Wisdom of Insecurity*. New York: Vintage Books, 1951.

White, Gordon. *Ani.Mystic: Encounters With a Living Cosmos*. n.p.: Scarlet Imprint, 2022.

Wohlleben, Peter. *The Hidden Life of Trees: What They Feel, How They Communicate: Discoveries from a Secret World*. London: William Collins, 2017.

Wright, Charles. *Black Zodiac*. New York: Farrar Straus Giroux, 1997.

Yeats, W.B. *Selected Poems*. New York: Gramercy Books, 1992.

Yunkaporta, Tyson. *Sand Talk: How Indigenous Thinking Can Save the World*. New York: HarperOne, 2020.

To Write to the Author

If you wish to contact the author or would like more information about this book, please write to the author in care of Llewellyn Worldwide Ltd. and we will forward your request. Both the author and publisher appreciate hearing from you and learning of your enjoyment of this book and how it has helped you. Llewellyn Worldwide Ltd. cannot guarantee that every letter written to the author can be answered, but all will be forwarded. Please write to:

Nathan M. Hall
⅄ Llewellyn Worldwide
2143 Wooddale Drive
Woodbury, MN 55125-2989

Please enclose a self-addressed stamped envelope for reply,
or $1.00 to cover costs. If outside the U.S.A., enclose
an international postal reply coupon.

Many of Llewellyn's authors have websites with additional information and resources. For more information, please visit our website at http://www.llewellyn.com

Notes